SOCIAL MEDIA SUPER SUCCESS

The psychology and techniques for using social media to grow your business

Sam Flynn

Copyright

Title: Social Media Super Success

First published in 2017 by SF2 Ltd.

Address: 217a Finney Lane, Heald Green, Cheshire, SK8 3PX

Website: www.samflynn.com

ISBN: 9781549626708

For press and publicity, contact the author.

Author address: 217a Finney Lane, Heald Green, Cheshire, SK8 3PX

For Ella and Sienna

Acknowledgements

Thanks firstly to you, the reader, for taking the time out to purchase and (hopefully!) read my book. I really, truly hope this book impacts your business. Don't forget, knowledge is useless without implementation!

To Daniel Priestly. You don't know me. Maybe one day you will! But reading your book 'Key Person of Influence' was the driving factor for me in deciding to write a book. If you haven't read Key Person of Influence, or any of Daniel's books for that matter, then do!

To Alice, thank you for listening to me whinge for the past however many years it has been that we've been meeting to drive our businesses forward! For encouraging me to keep meeting my objectives, and for giving me belief in myself.

To Ginny, for analysing my manuscript and for your great advice.

To Mike, for proof-reading the final draft and giving great improvement suggestions.

To my girls, Ella and Sienna, for giving me the drive to keep going with this career of mine. And for encouraging me to chase my dreams so that I can spend more time with you while you're still young enough to want to spend time with your mum!

And mostly, to Sean. For constantly asking how the book is coming along, and pushing me along the way. For always believing in me. For listening to my rants and thoughts. For coming back with the best ideas. For keeping me sane. And for being my best friend.

Table of Contents

Introduction

Social media is no longer that 'thing' you may, at some stage, consider using for your business. Nor is it something you'd completely discounted as only being for Justin Bieber fans! If you're not using social media for your business, then you're missing out! With huge volumes of users on each platform, chances are your target market will be amongst them; on at least one of the platforms. In reality, there are few categories of target market that are not now represented on a social media platform.

If you are new to social media for business, then this book should help guide you in starting out the right way. Or you may have been using social media for some time for your business, are yet to see the success that others report they are experiencing, and you're wondering why. I hope, if that's you, this book will help you too! Or you may be seeing lots of success on social media, but there are areas of it you have yet to explore, or you want to catapult that success. Then I really hope you find some nuggets in here for you as well!

The one thing I really want for all my clients, and now my book readers too, is social media super success. However, that comes from much more than attending a training course, or reading a book. Success comes from action! I'd advise you to treat yourself to a nice new notebook (I love the promise of a fresh, new notebook!). This notebook can be the place to keep all your social media notes, starting with those you make from this book. Jot down anything you think is relevant to your business, any actions you want to take, timescales you want to set yourself, page numbers you need to look back on, and anything else that pops in to your head as you read through the book (social media related of course, not what you plan to have for your dinner!). Then, in the future, you can refer to that book, ticking off the actions you've implemented. And you can add to the book, as you learn more about social media. It is forever changing after all.

Each section within the book focuses on a different area of social media marketing. The content for each section is typically not platform specific, and can be applied to each platform. There are also some platform specific uses included but there isn't a lot of technological detail about where to click. This is much more about the psychological way in which businesses can use social media. Luckily, there is a great tool you may have heard of that can quickly give you guidance on how to do the technology side. That tool is called Google (or any other search engine for that matter! Don't worry, that isn't the pinnacle of the tool suggestions!). A quick search will show you the steps to taking technological actions. But it's not always so easy to figure out how to do the business-building side of social media. That's what this book will deliver!

Enjoy the book, and I wish you lots of social media success!

My Story

When asked what I wanted to be when growing up, I used to say a teacher, but the reality was I really didn't know. I suppose, in some ways, I am a teacher, but social media didn't even exist when I was at school, so I could never have expected my career to be what it is today.

I grew up in the Isle of Man, moving over to England to study at university at 18 years old. I did a degree in Psychology, and decided to follow it up with a Masters in Organisational Psychology, in which the focus is on getting the most from people within business – coaching, employee engagement, training, recruitment, and so on. I spent my early twenties considering what career route to go down. Having spent time working in recruitment, Human Resources, in Canada, and then a brief spell as assistant to an HR Consultant, I decided I really wanted to work for myself.

I started my first business at 24 years old. I had helped construct an employee survey during one of my roles, and had focused a lot on testing and statistics in my Masters, so decided to start an employee survey company, Personnel Surveys, managing the employee survey process for organisations. I got a business loan, put it all on a website, and thought that was it. The phone would ring off the hook and the business would be an overnight success! Of course, it wasn't that easy, and I soon realised I needed to get marketing savvy. It didn't matter how well I did employee surveys, if I didn't market the business effectively, it wasn't going to work!

One of the things I focused a lot on was the use of LinkedIn to get in front of HR Managers. I invested in social media training and found it so interesting. I realised how much psychology was involved, in building effective business relationships through social media that convert in to customers. I pursued my passion of social media, learning as much as I could about it, and applying my own psychology knowledge to it. Within a year of setting up Personnel Surveys, I decided to set up a small sideline business – Sam Flynn Social Media. That is when things turned on their head very quickly!

Sam Flynn Social Media is now my main business. I have been training businesses in social media and speaking at business events about the use of social media, for 7 years. I use a lot of psychology in my approach, and you will notice this as you read this book. Social media success really isn't about the technology. It's about how you can engage people effectively, and build relationships with them, that ultimately make them want to buy from you again and again. I deliver in-house training for organisations, group workshops, and online training, as well as speaking at business events across the world on the effective use of social media for businesses. My clients have ranged from large international technology firms, to owner-managed businesses.

And my business has grown through my own social media use. I get 90% of my speaking gigs via LinkedIn, and around 70% of my business is generated via social media, predominantly LinkedIn and Twitter. I have the same struggles as other businesses. Time constraints being the main one, with two young girls to eat up my time too! But I know I must put the effort in on social media to help me grow my business and reach my goals. I truly hope this book will be a useful resource for you in helping you achieve social media super success!

CHAPTER 1

SOCIAL MEDIA STRATEGY

1.1. Why Do You Need A Social Media Strategy?

I'm not a huge fan of the word strategy. It sounds incredibly official, doesn't it?! I think the word itself can sometimes put people off creating a strategy. Essentially, a strategy is just a plan. Rather than delving straight in to social media without any real thought for how you're going to do it, start with a plan of what you're going to do, and what you want to achieve from it.

A strategy can have numerous purposes:

1. Company buy-in
If you receive push back from other people within the business, a strategy can help bring them round to your way of thinking. It will help them to understand why the company needs to use social media and the impact it may have, as well as the approach that will be undertaken.

2. Manage costs
A strategy will help you see where you need to spend money on your social media activity.

3. Manage resources
It will also help highlight other resources which you may need to involve with the social media activity.

4. Something to measure against
What is it you want to achieve on social media? Without objectives, it is hard to measure success.

5. Knowing who you want to reach on social media
A strategy can help you understand who, exactly, it is that you're targeting on social media.

6. Knowing what you want to say

I've worked with so many businesses, who decide that morning, what they're going to put out on social media, without having any content plan in place.

7. Planning for negativity

What are you going to do when a customer complains on social media? How will you manage your response? A strategy can cover this.

These are really, just a taster of the reasons. You may have many more that are specific to your company. The important thing is that you get a social media strategy in place.

1.2. What Should Your Strategy Include?

Your social media strategy can be completely designed around your business. You shouldn't be able to transfer your strategy from your business to a completely unrelated one. As such, your strategy should really contain elements that are important to your business. There are some features, however, that will be present in all strategies.

1. Social Media Objectives
2. Social Media KPIs
3. The Platforms You Will Focus On
4. Target Audience
5. Content Plan
6. Engagement Plan
7. Resources and Tools
8. Social Media Advertising
9. Measuring Success

Let's explore each of these sections in more detail...

1.3. Social Media Objectives

Taking a gung-ho approach, and diving head first into social media, is not the best way to ensure your success! You are far more likely to see success on social media if you know what that 'success' is. Different businesses will want different outcomes from their social media activity. Some may have several outcomes that they are aiming for, while others may only have one.

The important thing is that you have a reason for doing it beyond, "because we should"! Once you know what your reason is, you can plan your approach around that objective. It becomes much easier to measure whether your social media is working, and to change your approach if it isn't. There are thousands of objectives you may have for your social media activity, but these are some of the more common ones:

- Increase brand awareness
- Improve brand reputation
- Increase traffic to the website
- Increase blog readers
- Increase sales
- Increase leads
- Back up marketing campaigns
- Increase PR opportunities
- Be seen as thought-leaders and experts
- Improve customer loyalty
- Increase average customer spend
- Respond more efficiently to customer queries
- Increase footfall
- Increase event attendance
- Increase referrals
- Open up more joint partnership opportunities

It would be easy to look at the above list and decide that you'd like to achieve them all. But your objectives wouldn't be specific enough if you did that, and you may find you don't achieve any of them. Instead, try to pick your top three objectives. The three that will have the biggest impact on your business. Then plan your strategy around those objectives. You may find you end up achieving the others as a by-product.

1.4. Social Media KPIs

Once you have your objectives in place, you then need to put numbers alongside them. It's easy to say we want to increase brand awareness, but how does that translate in to something that we can measure? Or that we want more web traffic: but what's more? One more visitor a week? One more a day? One an hour? One a minute? We need Key Performance Indicators (KPIs) in place to put numbers behind the objectives.

Your KPIs could be specific numbers. For example, you could say you want an extra 1000 web visitors every month. Or they could be percentages. You might want to increase Twitter followers by 5% each month, for example. The important thing is that there is a specific measure that you can measure against. And that it is time-bound and there is a deadline for achieving that KPI.

While some objectives are easy to translate in to KPIs, such as web traffic or sales, others are not so. How do we measure brand awareness for example? Survey people on the street to find out if they've heard of our brand?! You need to translate that objective in to something you can measure relatively easily each month, that will give you an indicator of whether you are meeting that objective.

For brand awareness, you may look at mentions on the social media platforms you are using. You can assume more people are aware of you if there are more people talking about you. You could also measure your follower numbers. The more followers you have on each platform, the more people who are aware of your business. For improvement in reputation, you may want to look at a percentage decline in complaints. Or look at tools that help you measure positive sentiment, which will analyse mentions of your business, to see whether they are positive or negative. For customer loyalty, measure how many times the same customer purchases from you. There is always a way to measure, sometimes you just need to think a bit deeper!

Your KPIs don't have to be set in stone. They can be adjusted as required. And you may not know whether your KPI is achievable, or not, until you have some activity taking place. Set them anyway, and review them each month, until you think you've hit the right KPIs that are achievable, but also push your activity.

1.5. The Platforms You Will Focus On

Unless you have a team of people managing the social media in your business, it can be very difficult to have a successful presence on a large number of platforms. What usually happens, when a business decides they need to be on every social media platform, is that they don't see success on any of them. They've spread their resources too thin. It is much better to pick the right platforms for your business and your target audience.

There is a section later in this book for each of the main social media platforms. It will highlight to you, what you can do on the platform, and the demographics of the users of that platform. Use this information to guide you as to the best platforms for your business. You will also need to consider the time and resource you have. You may highlight five platforms that would work well for your business, but have only twenty minutes a day to spend on social media. Chances are, you're not going to have a strong presence on five platforms in such a short space of time.

You could also prioritise the platforms. This will allow you to focus on the most important platform for your business first. Once you have established a good following on that platform, and have got in to a routine of creating content for it, you could then turn your attention to the next platform on your list. This is especially important if your time and resource is already stretched.

1.6. Your Target Audience

Before you do anything on social media, you need to know who it is that you're doing it for! If your target audience is CEO's of large multinational organisations, and you're attracting teenage Justin Bieber fans, then you're not getting it right (apart from the small percentage that are CEO teenage JB fans!). You need to know who your audience is, so that you can deliver content that attracts them to follow your brand on social media.

For a large majority of businesses, the target audience is likely to be the same as the target market. The people we wish to become customers of our brand. For others, it may be people who can help us get to our target market. But, whoever that audience is, it needs to be defined.

You need to answer the following questions to help highlight exactly who that audience is, and to help form your content.

- Are they a consumer or a business?
- If it's a business, who, within that business, is the person you need to speak to (e.g. Marketing Manager, HR Director, Facilities Manager, etc.)?
- Are they a specific gender?
- What age range are they likely to fall in to?
- Where is their location?
- For a business focused audience, what industry are they in? What is their turnover? How many employees do they have?
- Any defining aspects that specifically make them your target market (e.g. pregnant, applying for university, business start up)?
- What are their interests?
- What makes them happy?

- What problems are they looking to overcome?
- What content do they consume?
- What knowledge are they looking for?
- How could you make their life easier?

Explore these and any other questions you think might be important in understanding who your target audience is. This will not only help you find them on social media, and highlight the platforms that they are using, but it will also help form your content.

1.7. Content Plan

Your content is likely to be the most important aspect of your social media activity. It is what draws people to follow you on social media, and to engage with you. It will help to build the relationship with your audience and, ultimately, it will hopefully encourage them to buy from you. So, if there's one thing you certainly need to have a plan for, it's your content!

Your content should align with the objectives you have set for your social media activity. For example, if you want more web traffic, your content will occasionally need to send them to your website! It also needs to be relevant for your target audience, and we'll explore this in more detail in the content section.

Your content can take many forms, and focus on many different themes. Your content plan should highlight what those forms and themes are. What imagery will you use? Will you create videos? Will you write blog posts to send your audience to? How will you generate leads through your content? These questions, along with many others, are what your content plan should answer. Once you have an overall plan for your content, you will be able to refer to this each time you create content. As such, you should never be stuck for something to say on social media!

Your content plan may also include an editorial calendar. Are there any seasonal events you can exploit with your content, such as Christmas, Easter, Valentine's Day, Mother's/Father's Day, etc. Or annually celebrated days, such as National Selfie Day! Are there any annual events that take place within your business? Do you have new product or service releases coming up within the year that you need to plan content for? Do you have any events you are attending? Any charity fundraisers? Having all of this in your editorial calendar for the year, allows you to plan your content in advance, for that event. You could create this on a spreadsheet, a calendar, or write it out on a wall planner, whatever works best for you.

Your content plan should be a work in progress. On most platforms, you can measure the 'success' of your content in terms of the reach and engagement. You should use this information to guide you in the content that is working for your audience, and the content that isn't, and keep adjusting your plan as required.

1.8. Engagement Plan

Engagement is so important on social media. It's what leads to the relationship between you and your audience, and ultimately, to them becoming a customer. It's why I've committed a section of this book to engagement, and it's why you need to include an engagement plan in your strategy.

Your engagement plan should outline how you are going to increase engagement and how you are going to manage that engagement. Will you reply to every comment? How will you respond if someone likes your tweet? Will you praise people for sharing your posts? How will you increase engagement? Will you seek out other users and engage with their content, or just engage with responses on your own content?

The more we engage on social media, it is highly likely the more success we will have. You need to plan how you can engage with your audience, with the time that you have available.

1.9. Resources and Tools

Once you understand more about the platforms you are going to use, and the content you are going to share, then you will start to highlight additional resources and tools that you need.

Your resources could include:

People:
- Additional manpower to manage the social media
- Photographer
- Graphic designer
- Videographer
- Copywriter

Media:
- Images
- Videos
- Graphics

Tools:
- Management tools
- Measurement tools
- Content tools
- Advertising tools

You will probably need to update this as your activity increases. We'll explore more of the tools available throughout the book, and you may also find it helps you highlight a need for additional resource.

1.10. Social Media Advertising

While much of the activity you can do on social media is free (beyond the use of your time), there is also the opportunity to advertise on most platforms. These adverts typically take one of two forms – sponsoring your content, and pay-per-click, or pay-per-impression, adverts.

With the large audience numbers using social media, it is a brilliant place to advertise. Nearly every business can benefit from social media advertising. With the sophistication in targeting options, it's definitely something to try.

So, what do we need to consider for our strategy?

- How will social media advertising support the rest of our activity?
- How can it help us achieve our objectives?
- What kind of adverts will we look to use?
- Which platforms will we advertise on?
- Who will we target with our adverts?
- What outcomes do we want from our adverts?
- How will measure the return on investment?
- What return on investment are we aiming for?
- What will our initial budget be?
- What imagery/videos can we use in our advertising?
- What landing pages will we send them to?
- Will we sell directly in our adverts?
- Will we use them to generate leads?
- Which content are we typically going to sponsor, to reach a wider audience?

Just as social media advertising could be a large book on its own, it could also form its own strategy within your business. You may also want to omit this from your strategy until you are ready to start advertising on social media and you have more of an understanding of it.

1.11. Measuring Success

I have worked with so many businesses who have never done any measurement of their social media activity. Each month, they continue doing what they are doing without any real idea of whether it's working or not. They could be completely wasting their time. Or stood on top of a gold mine without realising it!

Again, the importance of this step in your strategy means that there is a whole section in this book dedicated to social media measurement and how to do it. So, have a read of that before you formulate your measurement strategy.

Your measurement strategy will need to align with your objectives and KPIs, to allow you to see if you are achieving them. Things you may want to answer in your strategy include:

- Which platforms will we measure activity on?
- What specifically will we measure (e.g. followers, mentions, shares, replies, complaints, web traffic, sales, leads, etc.)
- What tools will we need to help measure these?
- How will we report our findings?
- How will we use this information to improve our social media activity?

1.12. CASE STUDY – RED BULL

Red Bull are often cited as social media champions. You should definitely go and check them out, particularly on Facebook where they have their biggest following, with over 47.8m page likes at the time of writing.

Red Bull's strategy focuses much more on building an engaged community on social media than on selling energy drinks. You will see from their content that they have figured out what works best for their audience. They focus predominantly on sports, particularly extreme sports. They use a lot of video content, with each getting tens of thousands of views, and lots of engagement on the post. They have analysed who their audience is and what their audience wants. They then keep adapting their content based on the feedback of their audience, such as looking at which videos get the highest views and engagement levels.

If Red Bull were to focus their content on their energy drinks, would they have anywhere near as much social media success? I can be pretty sure that the answer would be NO! They have moved away from their product to build an engaged following, that will ultimately help to build their brand awareness, and impact sales of their products.

Red Bull also take time to engage with their audience, responding to comments. This is something which isn't generally that common with larger brands. Red Bull have incorporated engagement in to their strategy, making their audience feel valued and part of the Red Bull community.

It's easy to look at a company like Red Bull and think 'it's ok for them'! Yes, they are a well-known multinational brand. But the important thing is to look at why their social media works. You probably don't need millions of social media followers to meet your social media aims. Look at successful brands on social media and consider the strategy they have adopted and why it has worked for them. Then look at how you can apply a similar strategy in your business.

In this case, I'd be asking whether focusing on product or service is the best approach within your social media strategy. It may be that you need a different focus that will help build your brand awareness, just as Red Bull have done. You need to understand who your audience is and what is going to work best for them. You also need to consider the best media approach for your audience. Are they more likely to watch video content than read updates? And finally, measure the response, using the data to improve your strategy going forward.

1.13. SUMMARY

- Create a social media strategy for your business, to outline the approach you will take on social media and why you are doing it
- Be clear on your objectives and translate these in to key performance indicators
- Outline the platforms you are going to focus on and who your audience is
- Include content themes and approaches
- Add how you are going to engage with your audience
- Think about the resources and tools you have available to you or may need to invest in
- Add a section on how you will use social media advertising for your business
- We can only be sure our activity is successful if we measure. Include how you will measure your activity

WANT MORE?

You can find a strategy template to download and fill in by heading to www.samflynn.co.uk/bookresources.

CHAPTER 2

SOCIAL MEDIA PLATFORMS

2.1. Choosing Your Platforms

There are so many social media platforms out there now. Unless you have a large social media team working every day on your social media, chances are it's not worth you being on all of them. It's likely you'll get more success from social media if you do a small number of platforms really well, than lots of platforms poorly.

I get around 70% of my business through my social media activity. But the majority of this is from LinkedIn and Twitter, and so these platforms are where I focus the majority of my time. It wouldn't make sense for me to spend as much time on Facebook and Instagram, where I get fewer business opportunities.

When choosing which platforms to use, the main thing to consider is which platforms your target audience use. There is no point using platforms, that the people you want to absorb your content, are not using. To understand which platforms your audience use, you could ask your current customers. Send them a survey asking which social media platforms they use the most. Then use that information.

You can also look at the key demographics for each platform (you should be able to find these by doing a quick Google search). Alternatively, you could run a dummy advert on that platform, going through your demographic options and seeing how many people fit those demographics on that platform.

And you can renew this regularly. If you are not seeing any success on a platform, consider whether it is because your target audience aren't using it. Be wary though, as it may be that you content is not appealing to them and that you need to change that, rather than abandon the platform altogether.

Think about the time you have available as well. If the time you have for social media is limited, consider just using one platform to maximum effect than spreading that time between several platforms. If you have a person or team dedicated to social media, then the chances are that you will have more opportunity, to use more platforms effectively.

2.2. Facebook

Facebook is probably the one we first think of when it comes to social media. Facebook currently has 1.86 billion active monthly users (users who have logged in within the last 30 days). It is the leader in terms of user numbers and, chances are, your target audience are using it.

Facebook users each have their own personal Facebook profile. When Facebook first started to grow, businesses were keen to get involved and some set themselves up with their own personal profile. This led Facebook to launch Facebook Pages, which allowed businesses to create their own presence on Facebook without having to pretend to be a person and add friends.

Users can choose to 'like' your Facebook page. This means they are more likely to see your content in their Facebook newsfeed. There are, however, issues with reach, which mean that not all users that like your page will see your content (more on this can be found in the content section). Be wary of choosing to set up your business as a personal profile. This is against Facebook terms, and they will remove your profile if they discover it.

On Facebook pages, you have several options for your content. You can simply use words, add images, videos, 360° images and videos, go live, share clickable links, check in to a location, create events and share offers. Users can interact with your content by commenting on updates, liking them, sharing them with their own audience, clicking on your links and watching your videos. They can also send you a message via Facebook that you are then able to respond to privately. You can add an about section, including web site links, opening hours and location. You can also include a call to action, such as 'learn more', 'call now' or 'watch video'. And you can open your page to customer feedback by allowing reviews on your page.

2.3. Instagram

Instagram has found its way up to the number two spot when it comes to the main social media platforms, overtaking Twitter in terms of monthly active use. Use is typically dominated by younger generations, with over half of Instagram users being under 30, though it is slowly emerging in to the over 30 category too.

Instagram is, a mobile-dominant, social media platform. The majority of activities, that you can perform, take place via the mobile app. You set up your Instagram profile on the app, and can only post to Instagram via the app. You can follow, view, like and comment via the desktop version.

Instagram is a photo and video sharing platform. You cannot post an update unless you have a photo or a video, up to 1 minute in length, to add to it. You can add up to 2200 characters to accompany your photo or video. You can amass followers, who will then see your updates within their Instagram feed. This is related to what they are most interested in, and what others have responded to, so they may not see all your updates as a result. Users can like your updates and comment on them. There is no sharing option on Instagram itself, though there are apps that allow you to share (or regram) Instagram posts. You cannot add links within your posts, but you can add a link in your profile, along with up to 150 characters about you and a profile picture.

2.4. Twitter

Twitter differentiates itself from the other social media platforms by being a 'micro-blogging' site. Updates are limited to 140 characters, so you need to be a lot more succinct in what you say!

Users choose to follow other users, while amassing followers themselves. Followers then see the Twitter updates (tweets) of the users they are following in their Twitter feed. They can like the update, reply to it, share it (retweet), and retweet it with a quote of their own, and they can watch videos and click on links within that update. Users can share images with their updates, GIFS, polls, and videos up to 2 minutes and 20 seconds long (140 seconds – do you see a theme emerging?!).

You can also send another user a private direct message, as long as that user is following you (to cut back on spam messages). You can search for keywords, or hashtags, used within tweets, and you can add users to lists, that allow you to see the updates of those that you add to a list within one stream.

2.5. LinkedIn

LinkedIn is commonly regarded as the more professional of the social media platforms. It is very much focused around your career or business, and is dominated by the working world rather than the social world.

Most of the activity on LinkedIn centres around your personal profile. You create your profile based on your work experience and your current role. You can then build connections, by sending connection requests to other users and accepting connection requests that you receive. You can post status updates on LinkedIn that are seen on the home feed of your connections. People can like, comment on and share these updates. You can also publish posts on LinkedIn. These are articles hosted on LinkedIn, with a title, an image and the main text, which people can also comment on, like and share.

You can also send messages directly to those people you are connected to. You can participate in groups with individuals, opening discussions and liking and commenting on the discussions of others.

And there is a more company-focused area to LinkedIn too, in the form of company pages. These give details about the company, and allow the company to share updates on the news feed of those who wish to follow the company. Again, users can like, comment on and share these updates.

2.6. Pinterest

Pinterest is an online bookmarking tool. It allows you to save content from the web on to pinboards that you have created, based around specific themes. You can also load images to pinboards without having to include a link.

You can create as many pinboards as you wish. Users can follow your whole Pinterest profile, or can choose to follow specific boards that you have created. They will see your content for the boards that they follow (or all content, if they have followed you as a user) in their Pinterest feed. They can choose to save this content to their own Pinterest boards, like it, mark it as 'tried it', comment on it, and send it on to someone, or another social media platform.

You can add a description to your pin, using up to 500 characters. While Pinterest does tend to be mostly visual, you can also pin videos via hosting sites such as YouTube and Vimeo. Pinterest has a browser extension, allowing you to pin directly from websites that you visit.

2.7. Snapchat

Snapchat allows you to send pictures and videos to your Snapchat contacts, or add them to your story. Your story can be viewed by all users who have chosen to follow you on Snapchat. All snaps expire after 24 hours and can no longer be viewed (though you can save your own snaps to your phone, and other users can screen grab them). This means there is no history of your previous snaps prior to 24 hours earlier.

You can doodle over your snaps, add stickers to them and add filters. You can also add geo-filters, which use your GPS information to give you the options of local filters, for example, giving town or location information. You can also apply lenses to faces, such as a dog face, which sticks a tongue out every time you open your mouth! As such, you can probably imagine that Snapchat use is dominated by the younger generations. It's a fun platform, and is great for building the story of your working day.

If you choose to allow it, your followers can chat to you in response to your snaps.

2.8. YouTube

YouTube is a social media platform itself. You can create a channel for your business, with categories and playlists to organise the videos you upload. People can choose to subscribe to your channel, and notified when you upload videos. And they can also click to like or dislike your video, as well as comment on it.

Video is so important in social media. If you are creating video content for social media, it makes sense to load it to a YouTube channel as well. YouTube content can be found through both Google and YouTube search, so your videos can be discovered years after they have been uploaded.

Be sure to add a description to each video that states what the video is about, and includes links to your other social media platforms, your website and any contact details you wish to include.

YouTube is also useful for hosting videos to be embedded on your website. If you would like to create video blogs (or vlogs), you can upload these to your YouTube channel and then embed them within a blog post.

2.9. CASE STUDY – CURTINS

Curtins are a multi-award winning consultancy, specialising in the built environment. With Curtins being a business-to-business organisation, they have decided not to focus their attention on every platform available to them.

Instead, Curtins only have a presence on LinkedIn and Twitter, sharing regular updates on both platforms. They keep their audience up to date with progress on their projects, awards that they have been nominated for, and have won, interesting articles and what their team are up to.

Your audience, be it either businesses or consumers, should guide your decision as to where to make use of your social media resources. For business-to-business organisations, LinkedIn and Twitter will usually be the platforms that can provide the most success when used correctly. It can be much harder to see success on more consumer-driven platforms like Facebook and Instagram. While of course, it would be great to be using all platforms, all day, for most businesses this isn't an option. So, picking those platforms your audience are predominantly using is a much wiser strategy.

Curtins, like many business-to-business companies, have avoided using Facebook. Similarly, many consumer-led businesses avoid using LinkedIn for marketing purposes. It's important to think about where you are most likely to build relationships with your target audience. Some business-to-business companies have great success on Facebook and Instagram. It very much depends on what kind of businesses you are looking to target, again bringing it back to your audience. Knowing your audience and researching the platforms that they are most likely to use is key.

2.10. SUMMARY

- You don't have to use every social media platform available to you
- Choose the platforms to be present on based on those your audience use and the time you have available
- Understand the advantages of each platform for your business
- Consider the most popular platforms, including Facebook, Instagram, Twitter, LinkedIn, Pinterest, Snapchat and YouTube

WANT MORE?

You can find a pros and cons template for each social media platform at www.samflynn.co.uk/bookresources.

CHAPTER 3

YOUR SOCIAL MEDIA PROFILES

3.1. Your Header Image

Most of the platforms allow you to add a large image across the top of your profile. Each will have its own size requirements, and the platform should tell you what that size requirement is. Alternatively, you can use Canva.com, which has templates for social media images, including the header image on the main platforms. You can also add text over the top of images using Canva.

Your header image really stands out on your profile pages. It is the image the eye is drawn to first, and will pull in both new and returning visitors to your profile. It may even form their decision on whether to look through your profile or leave it. It doesn't need to be static. In fact, it's worth changing your header image regularly to keep it interesting and relevant.

Here are a few ideas of what your header image could be:

- Your logo (if not using it for your profile picture)
- A shot of your team
- A picture of your premises
- A behind-the-scenes internal look at your business premises
- Fun things that have happened in your business, such as fancy dress days
- Pictures of your product(s)
- Pictures of your service in action
- Seasonal imagery (e.g. Christmas, Easter, Valentines, Summer, etc.)
- A promotion
- Photo competition entries
- An eye-catching graphic

Fit it with your branding, using the same kind of colours and fonts. Try to avoid too much use of text. Keep the focus on the imagery.

3.2. Your Profile Picture

Most social media platforms require a profile picture. It's not mandatory. But for business success on social media then it absolutely is mandatory.

This is a very important image. It sits alongside each of your updates. It represents your business. And yet most businesses give it very little thought. They see the requirement for a picture and immediately upload their logo, not thinking twice about it. They rarely even resize that image to make sure it is completely in focus.

Your logo is an obvious choice for your profile picture. It's your business' branding. It's on your website, your business cards, your email signatures. And for some businesses, it is completely right that the profile picture should be the business logo. Imagine Nike using anything other than the recognisable tick. Or Coca-Cola working for weeks to uncover their perfect social media profile picture, when they've already got one of the most renowned logos in the world. The problem is that, unless you are reading this as an employee of Nike, Coca-Cola, McDonalds or any of the other big international companies we immediately know the logo of, your customers don't know your logo. What's more, they don't really care about it either. If I asked you to describe the logos of 10 different small businesses, you'd probably struggle.

The logo is not always the best option. A logo immediately identifies your social media accounts as being business-focused. And, as a result, your audience may scan over your updates looking for those from 'real people'. They may also be deterred from following you back when you follow them, as they see your approach as being nothing more than a business who wants to sell to them. They can't relate to your logo. They are unlikely to remember your logo.

Sometimes, the better solution is a face. Someone who they can remember. Who they associate with that business. A person whom they will read the updates of, rather than skip over. A face that makes your social media far more 'social', as it means talking to a real person, rather than a corporate machine. Certainly, if you're like me, a business in which people refer to you and your name, more than they do the business name, then the profile picture should absolutely be your face. I regularly get professional pictures taken for social media profile use.

In addition, you could look at other stand out options. A product. Or your service in action. A cartoon or doodle. Something that fits well with your brand but that helps you to stand out on social media.

Whatever you choose, a profile picture is an absolute must! Just make sure you think through the right option for your business.

3.3. Your Facebook Page

As well as your cover image and profile picture, there are some other areas of your Facebook page you need to pay some attention to. Think of your Facebook page as being another website for your business. Many users will go no further than your Facebook page, so make sure it gives them as much information as they possibly need about your business.

1. About and Description
The about section is visible on your Facebook page. You have 255 characters, so quickly get to the point of what your business does. Make it succinct and easy to understand. You could also add anything here that makes you special and stand out, if you have the space.

2. Call to Action
The call to action sits underneath the cover image on your Facebook page. Facebook gives you many options for this, including 'learn more' (directs them to a webpage of your choosing), "call now" (allows them to call direct from their mobile), "watch video" (sends them to a video you upload for them to watch), "book now" (link them to your booking page) and many others to choose from. Pick the one that you think is likely to get the best response from your audience. And use your insights to see how many people are clicking your call-to-action.

3. Location and Contact Details
Add your location and contact details so that visitors to your page can quickly get in touch.

4. Reviews
You can allow the option for visitors to leave you a review on your Facebook page. This can help other people see how great you are! It's also a really good way to engage with your customers on Facebook, allowing you to respond to their comments.

5. Opening Hours

Let people know the hours that you are open. It will state that you are closed on your Facebook page outside of these hours, which can be good for showing a response is unlikely at that time if you aren't able to manage your social media outside of your open hours.

6. Pinned Post

You can pin any of your posts so that they appear at the top of your Facebook page. Click the down arrow in the top corner of the post to pin that post to the top. Think of the first thing you want visitors to see on your page. This could be something you're promoting, a video you want them to watch, or a link you want them to click.

3.4. Your Twitter Profile

Look at your Twitter profile from the eyes of a new visitor. Would it encourage people to want to follow your business on Twitter? The first thing to think about is your Twitter username. While you can change this, I wouldn't change it regularly. It should be something which is easy for users to remember and that is relevant to your business. It could be as simple as using your business name, or you could use it to describe what your business does.

Then consider your 'full name' on Twitter. Again, you could simply use the business name. Or you could use the name of the person managing the account so that people know who they are talking to. For example, if your business name was XYZ, you could use 'Ben @ XYZ'.

For your bio, you have 160 characters of space to fill to tell people more about your business. Make sure you clearly state what the business does and maybe add a bit of your 'brandonality' in there too, if there is space.

Your location needs to state where you are based. Even if you sell worldwide, I would add a specific location, and that you are worldwide. E.g. Manchester and Worldwide.

And finally, your website. The obvious option is to send users to your website homepage. You could also consider creating a specific page for those who click through from Twitter. Alternatively, send them to something you are trying to promote at that time.

You can pin a Twitter update to the top of your page by clicking the down arrow in the top corner of your post. That post will then sit at the top of your profile, with the rest of your content appearing chronologically. Think about the first post you want visitors to your Twitter profile to see. It may be something you are currently promoting, or a video about what you do. You can change this at any time, by removing the pin, or pinning another update to the top of your profile.

3.5. Your Instagram Profile

Instagram is a little different to most of the other social media platforms in that you must create your profile on a mobile phone. Again, you will need a profile picture, and a short bio of 150 characters. Be sure to describe to people what they can expect from your Instagram feed. You should also add a link to your profile, as you are unable to add links to updates. You can change this link as often as you want. For example, if you wish to direct people to a certain link, you can change the link in your profile, and tell them within the update to click the link in your bio.

You can switch to a business profile on Instagram, by going to your settings and choosing to switch to a business profile. This will give you the option to add a contact button to your profile, which allows users to call, email and get directions to your premises via your profile. Switching to a business profile also means you will get access to Instagram insights, which allow you to measure your Instagram activity.

Instagram is a very visual experience. You can create a more fluid and attractive looking profile by using similar imagery throughout your profile. This could simply mean using the same filter for each image, or you could create a theme, such as including yellow in every image, or sharing only images of people on your Instagram account.

3.6. Your LinkedIn Profile

Much of LinkedIn's power lies in the use of your personal profile. While company pages are great for sharing updates, it can be difficult to grow a following, and you are limited with the activity you can do from your company page. There is much more functionality in the personal side of LinkedIn and it's also much easier to build relationships person to person than business to business.

Before you start connecting with people and engaging with them on LinkedIn, you want to make sure your profile is up to date. That is where they will go to find out more about you. So, there's no point putting in all the effort if it's not representing you well. There is a lot that you can add to your LinkedIn profile, but I'm going to talk about the most important sections for your LinkedIn success.

1. Your Profile Picture

Make sure it looks professional but also represents your personality. If you don't usually wear a suit and tie for work, then don't in your profile picture! Use a headshot rather than a full body. People only need to see your face. If possible, get a professional photographer to take it. This will give you a picture you can use across different forms of social media and marketing. No night out pictures!!

2. Your Headline

Your headline sits underneath your name on LinkedIn. It's the first suggestion of what it is that you do and it is visible on search results, giving the person searching, an indication of whether to click through to your profile or not. Make sure it clearly defines what the company is. You are using your LinkedIn profile to promote the company you work for. Make sure that you state, not just the company name, but what that company does. Telling me you're the Marketing Manager at XYZ Ltd will give me no clue as to what XYZ Ltd is.

3. Your Summary

This is where most people go in to CV mode. “I am hard working, conscientious, etc. with 20 years of experience, blah, blah”. Useful if you’re looking for a job. Not so useful if you’re looking to take on new clients and customers. Instead, start your summary by talking about the business and what it can do for someone reading your profile. Then move on to your role in that business, and finally a bit more about you.

4. Additional Media

You can add additional media to your summary, such as videos, images and PDFs. This is a great way to stand out that bit more, to add more information and to impress potential clients. If you have a video introducing your company, include it here. Or you could share a useful PDF or a stand out image.

5. Experience

This isn’t your CV remember. We don’t need to know about everything in your employment history. Try to keep it relevant to what you are doing now. Be sure to add a description to each role, especially your current role.

6. Contact Information

Don’t make it difficult for people to get in contact with you. Share the main company phone number and email address. Add a link to your website. There are three slots for websites on LinkedIn profiles, so use all three. If you only have one website, send people to three different pages on that website.

There is much more you can add to your LinkedIn profile, but these are the most important in marketing terms. Your LinkedIn profile is keyword searchable in LinkedIn search. Think about the keywords that your potential clients will be searching for that should lead to you as the solution. Then use those keywords throughout your profile, as much as you possibly can. The more times a searched keyword is present within your profile, the higher up in search results you will come (in combination with how connected you are to the person searching). This is how I generate 90% of my speaking gigs through LinkedIn. 'Social media speaker' is a keyword phrase that I appear in the top search results for.

3.7. LinkedIn Company Pages

Company pages on LinkedIn are another place for you to market your business on LinkedIn, and share updates. You can amass followers for your company page, who will then see your company updates in their LinkedIn feed. The functionality of a company page is much more limited than that of a personal profile. You cannot interact privately with a LinkedIn user as your company page, you cannot publish posts (articles), you cannot interact in groups, and you cannot like or comment on other updates on LinkedIn as your company. As such, personal profiles of employees can often be a more effective way to market your business on LinkedIn.

Company pages do offer a good opportunity to build a following of people interested in your company. It is a good place to share company-related updates and business-focused updates. Your followers can then interact with that content, commenting on and liking updates, as well as sharing them with their LinkedIn connections.

Be sure to fill out a full description of your company on the page, and think about the right header and profile image to attract people to follow your company page. Your company page can become a great forum for discussion. Open discussions by asking questions, and reply to comments to keep the conversation flowing.

It can be difficult to build company page followers. It is not as easy as sending out a connection request, and highlighting to that individual that you exist. Be sure to market your company page to encourage people to follow you, in the following ways:

- Include a link from your website
- Include a link in email signatures

- Ensure all employees have a link to the company page on their profile
- Encourage employees to share company page updates
- Share regular content
- Ask questions to encourage engagement, which will increase reach
- Direct followers from other social media platforms to also follow you on LinkedIn

3.8. CASE STUDY – STARBUCKS

I'm sure you don't need me to tell you who Starbucks are! They are clearly one to watch and learn from on social media. The one thing I love about Starbucks' social media activity, is the way that they change their cover images regularly on those platforms that allow you to do so.

Their cover images are also very seasonal on their regional pages. In Winter, you'll see snowy images with steaming mugs of hot chocolate, in Autumn it's all about the pumpkin spice, in Spring there are blossoms with refreshing iced coffees, and in Summer it's icy cold coolers. Go to their Facebook page or Twitter profile and I guarantee you'll instantly want a cup of whatever is in their cover image at the time! They get it just right for the weather at the time.

Changing your cover image regularly is an effective strategy for promoting popular products or services at that time, or supporting campaigns that you are working on. Your cover image change on Facebook will also appear on the timeline of some of your fans.

Starbucks also have a 'Sign Up' call to action on their Facebook page, allowing you to sign up for their rewards programme. And the page shows you where your nearest Starbucks can be found (handy when you're tempted by those cover images!).

On LinkedIn, Starbucks focus their profile more around their recruitment and careers. They talk about how employees are known as 'partners' and link to their careers page. Their posts also reflect the careers focus, and is a great employer branding profile.

Consider how you could take the ideas Starbucks have used and implement them in your own business. Are there seasonal opportunities to make changes to your imagery? Or opportunities to promote specific campaigns?

3.9. SUMMARY

- The header image on your profiles can be updated regularly. Consider seasonality or products/services you wish to promote at that time
- Your profile picture should not be changed as often. Your logo may not be the best option for this picture. You could use a headshot or an image that represents your business
- Include as much information about your business as possible on your social media profiles
- Make it as clear as possible what the business does
- Add relevant links in your profiles

WANT MORE?

There is a checklist for you to download of everything you need to think about including in your social media profiles over at www.samflynn.co.uk/bookresources.

CHAPTER 4

TARGET AUDIENCE AND FINDING THEM

4.1. Increasing Fans, Followers and Connections

We all want more fans, followers and connections on social media. The more we have, the bigger our audience is likely to be. So, how do we go about getting as many of the right audience members as we can, for each platform?

1. Post Updates
No one is going to follow a user that either never, or rarely, posts updates on that platform. The more often and regular your content, the more your audience will build. It is a bit of a chicken and egg situation. What comes first – the followers or the updates? In this scenario, it should certainly be the updates! If you're new to a platform, be sure to start posting as if you have millions of followers.

2. Use Hashtags
Your content will be found more easily if you use relevant hashtags within that content. Have a read over the hashtag part of the content section.

3. Know Your Audience
Your audience is more likely to build if you post content that is relevant for that audience. Be sure to know who the audience is that you are trying to attract, then post content that is relevant to that audience.

4. Engage
Get more people engaging with your content, and it will become visible to a wider audience. See the engagement section for more details.

5. Run Competitions
On some platforms, you can run competitions to encourage people to follow you. For example, on Twitter you could ask someone to retweet a tweet and follow you to be entered in to a draw. Due to Facebook's

competition guidelines, you are not allowed to incentivise someone to like your Facebook page.

6. Share Links To Your Profiles

Make sure that you have links in as many visible places as possible. On each form of marketing you send out, there should be details of where they can find you on social media. On your website, email signatures, posters in your premises, business cards, leaflets, letters, and anywhere else that you think would be beneficial!

7. Follow and Connect With Others

Another way to increase your audience is by following and connecting with others. However, this isn't possible on all platforms. For example, you can't find people directly on Facebook who will fit your target market and encourage them to like your page, other than through paid advertising. For those you can, there are more details on each platform and finding your target audience within this section.

8. Advertise For Followers and Fans

You can choose to advertise on each platform to gain more followers and fans. This will be covered in more detail in the advertising section.

4.2. Finding People To Follow on Twitter

One way to increase your Twitter following is to follow your target audience. Not all will follow you back, but a proportion of them are likely to, so long as you are posting regularly and often. You can find your target audience on Twitter in the following ways:

1. Search Hashtags or Keywords
You could find your target audience by running a search on Twitter. Think of the hashtags or keywords that your target audience will use in their updates. For example, a golf shop might search for anyone mentioning 'golf' or an accountant looking for local small businesses might search for those getting involved in localised business Twitter chats (e.g. #CheshireHour, #NorwichHour, etc.). You can choose to make the search advanced by clicking to filter the search, allowing you to search for the keyword/hashtag in a specific location.

2. Who Do They Already Follow?
Think about who your target audience might already be following on Twitter. This could be your competitors, other local businesses, other businesses who target the same audience as you and any publications that they might read. Find the Twitter accounts for these users by searching on Twitter or doing a Google search. You can then click on 'followers' on their profile to look through their followers and start following those you think are right for your audience.

3. Who Follows Them?
Similarly, you could think about who might be following your target audience. Are there any businesses that are likely to follow them? Head to the profiles of those that you think will be following your audience, and click 'following'.

4. What Do They Say in Their Bio?
You can search for keywords mentioned within the bio of Twitter users. Run a search for those keywords on Twitter, using Boolean

search operators where relevant (e.g. "marketing manager", marketing AND manager, marketing OR manager). Once again you can then filter this by a location. Click on people, once you have run your search, to find those with the relevant keywords in their bio. Think of the keywords that your target audience would have within their bio, such as 'mum', 'dad', 'engaged', 'owner', 'managing director', etc.

5. Search for Public Lists

You can look through the members of public lists on Twitter. For example, if your target audience was entrepreneurs in Birmingham, you may discover there are several public lists created named 'Birmingham Entrepreneurs'. Twitter doesn't have a facility to search for public lists. But you can find them via Google. You will need to use the following search term, adding the list name in the brackets: site:twitter.com inurl:lists <*list name*>. E.g. site:twitter.com inurl:lists <Birmingham Entrepreneurs>. You can then click to view the members of the list and work your way through following those that you wish to.

4.3. Finding People To Follow On Instagram

Finding other users to follow on Instagram can be a great way to build up your own following. You can find them using the following methods:

1. Search Hashtags
Run a search for the hashtags your target audience would use. For example, if you are targeting people in your local area, search your local area hashtag.

2. Search People
You can search for users using specific keywords that they may use in their bio. Add your search term to the search bar and click 'people' as your search option.

3. Think of Who They Already Follow
Have a think about who your target audience will already be following on Instagram. It could be your competitors, other local businesses, publications, or any businesses that target the same audience that you do. Find their profile on Instagram via search, and click on their followers to work your way through following them.

4. Think of Who Might Follow Them
Similarly, you can think of who might be following your target audience, find their profile and click on 'following' to work your way through, following those you believe to be the right audience members for you.

4.4. LinkedIn Search

The top search bar is useful for searching for people you know by name. But what if you want to run a search for your target market? What if you wanted to find HR Managers in Manchester, or Finance Directors in Loughborough, or Personal Assistants in Aberdeen?

To do this you will need to filter your search. You can do this by clicking on the search bar. On the right-hand side, you will have several options for filtering your search. For example, if you click on 'keywords', you have the option to add a title. You can also change the location to search in a certain location.

1. To find the name of a contact to call
If there is a company you wish to work with, and you want to contact the right person within that company, LinkedIn can provide you with the name of that contact.

2. To use in direct mail campaigns
If you wish to send out a direct mail campaign to those holding a specific job title within a certain location, LinkedIn advanced search could provide you with a list of names to send your campaign to.

3. To build your connections on LinkedIn
LinkedIn can be a great platform to build your network. By using search, you can find people that you wish to connect with and to be part of your network. Filter by selecting 2nd connections when searching so that you are not searching for those you are already connected to. Be sure to send them a message with your connection request, detailing why you wish to connect with them.

4.5. Connecting With People You Don't Know on LinkedIn

LinkedIn pushes users to only connect with people you know. And that strategy can work extremely well, by nurturing the relationships you've already formed. However, it can limit your network. Connecting with people you don't know is an excellent way of expanding your network and building relationships with people you wouldn't have the opportunity to, face-to-face.

The other bonus of connecting with people you don't know on LinkedIn is that you will have more connections! I can almost definitely guarantee that there are more people in the world that you don't know than people that you do!!! I could even go as far as to say there are more people in your local area that you don't know than those that you do.

And for each connection you add on LinkedIn, you add all their connections as second connections. Your network increases. When someone runs a search on LinkedIn, those who are first or second connections will come higher up in your results. The more connections you have, the more second connections you have, and the more search results you come higher up in!

The big draw for me though, in accepting connection requests that come in from people I do not know, is that I don't know what their agenda is in connecting with me. It may be that they want to sell to me, that they want to tap in to my network, or, that they want to recruit me. Indeed, the best-case scenario could be that they want to do business with me. That they've searched on LinkedIn for a social media trainer or speaker, and I've come up in the results, and they've sent a connection request. Many people will send a connection request without adding a note to it, choosing to send you a message after you have accepted the connection. I would have missed out on a crazy amount of business if I hadn't accepted connection requests from those I don't know!

Of course, you do need to be sensible with your 'ignore' or 'accept' choice. View their profile. Do they look legit? Would you feel happy being connected to them? If not, then by all means, ignore that request. But the way I look at it, is that the worst thing that can happen if I get it wrong, is that they start to send me messages that I don't want to receive. At which point I can just remove the connection and that's that. I'd far rather accept in the hope they want to do business, and to not miss out on that business, than to ignore, in case they send me a message!

LinkedIn is a huge business source for me, and by expanding my network and 'meeting' new people on there, I know it will continue to be so.

4.6. Influencer Marketing

Another way to attract potential customers to your brand on social media, is by utilising social media influencers. These are key influencers within certain industries who have a large social media following. Brands will pay influencers sums that typically reflect the size of their following. Someone with 1000 Instagram followers will charge a lot less than someone with 1m Instagram followers for a sponsored Instagram post!

There are influencers for all sizes of budgets. For example, children's brands often work with parent bloggers to promote their brand on social media. There are such a broad range of parent bloggers that some may be happy to post about the brand for a small return, such as a free low cost item, while others will expect the item plus payment for their post.

To find influencers in your industry, search relevant hashtags on Instagram or Twitter, such as #pbloggers for parent bloggers or #bbloggers for beauty bloggers, or search industry words. You can also use a site call Hashtagify.me, to search for the key influencers using a specific hashtag.

If you provide a free product or service, or pay an influencer for a post, then the influencer must state this in their post. This is usually covered by using the hashtags #ad, #spon or #sponsored.

If you wish to work with influencers, most will have a 'work with me' section on their website, or PR contact details on their profiles. Alternatively, you could work directly with PR agencies to find you influencers to work with.

4.7. CASE STUDY – PADDY POWER

When it comes to betting companies using social media, very few have a following even close to that of Paddy Power. With over 1.5m Facebook fans, over 90k on Instagram and over 600k Twitter followers, they are way ahead of their competition in terms of audience size. So, what have they done to grow such a big social media audience?

The most important thing that they have done is to understand exactly who their audience is. They know their audience (predominantly male football fans) through and through. And they know what works well for their audience. They speak their audience's language. And they focus predominantly on sharing humorous posts, in particular football related humour.

As a result, the posts get shared lots, leading to an even bigger growth in audience numbers. They also get lots and lots of engagement, particularly with people tagging their friends who they think will also find it funny. Paddy Power's team even take the time to respond back to some of the comments too.

Paddy Power aren't afraid to be authentic on social media. They don't take a 'professional' approach, and the result has been a huge success. They keep it authentic as they know that's what works for their audience and helps it to grow. They also don't sell a lot on social media. The primary focus of their posts is on entertaining rather than selling. The result is they are building a community with a strong relationship to the brand, which will have a big impact on attaining and retaining customers.

One of the most important approaches to building your audience is knowing exactly who that audience is and what they want to see on social media. Get the content right and the audience will follow.

4.8. SUMMARY

- Post regularly with content that is relevant and interesting to your audience to help build your following
- You can also use advertising to help grow your following, targeting the right audience for your business
- Search hashtags to find your audience
- Consider who they may already be following
- Run searches on LinkedIn, and consider connecting with people you don't know
- Influencer marketing can help get your brand in front of a larger audience on social media

WANT MORE?

You can download an audience persona template at www.samflynn.co.uk/bookresources.

CHAPTER 5

CONTENT

5.1. Your Content

Your content is so important on social media. It forms the heart of your activity. Your content is what attracts people to follow you on social media. It is what helps them build a relationship with your brand. It is what they engage with. Ultimately, it may encourage them to buy from you.

While the high volume of use of social media is great for your brand, as it means that your customers are more than likely going to be using it, it also means that you have a lot of competition when it comes to content. You could be in competition with their friends and family, celebrities, other businesses, funny videos and memes, and all sorts of other content that is delivered every day on social media to users.

As there is so much content we could be absorbing, we have become professional scrollers! Just like we may skim a newspaper's headlines to decide which articles to commit our full attention to, we are likely to decide very quickly whether to stop scrolling and read, or watch, a piece of content. So, it is vitally important that your content stands out straight away.

Over this section, we will explore some of the key features of your content, and some ideas you can incorporate to make your content stand out.

5.2. Brandonality

The more businesses that use social media, the harder we must work to stand out. If there is one thing that helps us to stand out from anyone else, it's our personality. No two personalities are identical, and that is true of brand personalities too. Or as I like to call it "BRANDONALITY".

Brandonality is the personality of your brand. It's what personifies your brand and helps it stand out from the noise. And every brand has a brandonality even if they haven't yet discovered what that brandonality is.

Your brandonality could be the personality of a person within your business. This is true regardless of the size of the business. Think of Virgin, and we think of a certain personality – a 'Bransonality'!! And for me, the brandonality of my business is simply my personality. There's no point me having one personality in business, and one when I'm not working. What you see is what you get!!

If your brandonality isn't a specific person, it could be the personality of your business as a whole. What do people experience when they walk through the doors of your business? Is it a calm relaxing place to be, or is there hustle and bustle? Are there regular jokes being shared or does everyone quietly get on with their work? Is the décor vibrant and stand out, or is it muted and laid back? Is there a buzz about new technologies, or a buzz about the latest reality show?

What do your customers experience when buying from your business? Are they addressed as sir/madam or on first name terms? Are they constantly being pleasantly surprised or reassured in knowing what to expect?

How do you want to be seen? Do you want people to talk about the vibrancy of your business, or would you prefer they focused on your professional nature? Are you associated with innovation or traditional practices?

Really delve deep in to your business to determine its brandonality. Ask as many questions of the business, the employees and the customers as you can to work out your exact brandonality. And then use this brandonality on social media. Use it to determine the type of content that works best for your business. Use it to determine your tone of voice. Use it to help you stand out and, be authentic. The more we are ourselves, the more authentic and 'real' we come across, and this is no different from businesses.

The final big advantage of using your brandonality on social media, is that it personalises your business. Your audience feel like they're listening to a person rather than a corporation. They feel that they can engage with you, because there is a person there to answer. And it really helps to build the relationship with your brand, as without personality, relationships rarely flourish!

5.3. Give Your Target Audience What They Want

When producing content for social media, businesses often make the mistake of thinking first of what they want to tell people. Which message is important that they get out to the world. What they want to say about their products or services. The important business broadcasts they think MUST be heard!

But while they are busy focusing on what they want to tell people, the businesses who are thriving on social media are those that focus on giving their target audience what they want. Their target audience is pulled in to their business by the content that they deliver. They want more. They wait for future content. They engage with it and share it with their peers. The organic reach is high and the relationships built with their audience doesn't just convert them in to customers; it converts them in to loyal customers who won't consider buying from rival brands.

Once you know who your target audience is, it's important to then ask what content your target audience would engage with, and how you can share similar content while still making it relevant to your business and industry. As seen in the previous case study, betting company Paddy Power don't focus their social media activity on the latest odds, or why people should gamble with them over rival betting firms. Instead they share sports humour, and funny videos and memes. They know who their target audience is and they deliver content that they will engage with.

But, how do you know what content your target audience want to consume? ASK THEM! Send a survey out to your customers, as I'm sure you want more people just like them! Incentivise their response by running a prize draw for all responses. Give them content themes and ask them what they'd most like to see.

And pay attention to your social media activity. Did one piece of content result in huge engagement, shares and likes, while another had zero response? Look at what is working for your audience and give them more of it. Don't keep pushing out content that no one engages with. Note that it's not working for your audience, and focus on the content that you do know leads to high levels of engagement.

5.4. Selling By Not Selling

We've all had that moment. We've just put the kids in the bath. Or we've got the dinner cooking. Or we've just sat down after a long day. Or it's Saturday morning at 8am and we're trying to enjoy a well-deserved lie in. And then the doorbell goes!

"Hello sir/madam, I just wondered if you had considered getting your windows updated? We're working in this area at the moment, and I see your windows could do with an upgrade. We can provide you with a quote...." and on and on it goes.

I wonder how many people stand there, on the threshold of their home, thinking 'hurray, this is exactly what I was thinking about at just this moment. I'm so glad this person came to my door right now'! Not many, I'm sure.

You see, in that moment, we're not there to buy. We're busy, there's household distractions, there's other stuff we need to do, or we just want to relax in our own home. At that moment, we're not there to buy. Plus, we have zero relationship with the person on our doorstep, trying to sell us windows we didn't think we needed. Instead of pulling you in, that person is pushing you away. You're thinking of the quickest way of getting rid of them. They are an annoyance rather than the glorious solution to all your problems!

This happens every day, hour and minute on social media. Companies push sales messages out to their audience, and expect them to buy. Yet, the people at the end of the computer/tablet/phone haven't gone on social media to buy. They've gone to chat to their friends, see what celebrities are up to, or maybe to promote their own business. Very rarely will your customers be using social media with the aim of seeing what they can purchase. As such, posting sales messages is the virtual equivalent of the door-to-door sales person. They are not there to buy right now, so you end up pushing them away.

I'm not saying never ever post a sales message on social media. Of course, there are times when it would be daft not to mention what you sell. We'll come on to that. But the majority of your content on social media should be non-sales driven. This is 'social' media. We want interaction. We want to attract people to our brand. We want to BUILD A RELATIONSHIP!

5.5. Imagery

Imagery is incredibly important on most social media platforms. Of course, you have platforms like Instagram where it's a necessity. But on the likes of Facebook, Twitter and LinkedIn, imagery can play a huge part in ensuring your content stands out and gets read.

Imagery doesn't have to consist of pictures you have taken. There are many free stock image sites that will provide you with brilliant free images you can use on social media. If you do a quick search for 'free stock images' you'll find lots of great sites. My personal favourite is www.pixabay.com. Just search for the main keyword of your update, and I'm sure you'll find an image to support it.

You can also create your own designs easily with the help of a free tool called Canva (www.canva.com). Canva is great for social media, as it already has the right sized templates for images on the different social media platforms. You can upload your own images or stock images, use Canva's own stock imagery (often these include a purchase fee) or use a coloured or patterned background. You can then add text on top of that imagery. This is a great way to exaggerate the purpose of your post, by repeating the content of the post within your image.

Of course, your own photography is important too, and I'd recommend getting a professional photographer to spend a few hours in your business taking shots. Images of your premises, your employees, behind-the-scenes action shots, your products or delivering your services, form a great bank for your social media updates. For each update, you can have a quick look in your image bank to see if you have a relevant image to support it. And, I'm sure you're never far from a wonderful device that will allow you to take some pretty good pics – your phone! Most smartphones now take great quality pictures, and there are numerous apps (such as VSCO) that can sharpen the image to make it look more professional.

I tested images recently on Twitter and found that, within an hour, I received 22 more clicks on a blog post update that had an image than on one without an image. It makes a BIG difference! So, be sure to include an image with each update.

5.6. Share Your Best Knowledge

I sell knowledge. I train businesses and speak at events. It's all knowledge-sharing. So, why would I give my best knowledge away for free when that is what my business is? Why not make them pay for it?

If we keep our best knowledge for our paying customers, and only share the low-level knowledge, or nothing at all, then it is very difficult to position ourselves as experts. Your customers will only be willing to buy from you if they think you're the experts.

This is particularly important if, like me, you sell knowledge. Your business will only expand if your customers believe you are the best in what you do and deliver the highest level of knowledge. Your social media is the perfect showcase for this. While I will share my best knowledge for free in my blog and on social media, you'd have to spend a lot of time to bring it all together yourself. Plus, you are seeing it generically, and having to apply it your business yourself, rather than getting the one-on-one support that comes from working with me.

Share tips and advice, write blog posts, share articles that give step-by-step guides, record tutorial videos, create reports, get infographics designed, and do whatever else it takes to get your knowledge out there. Being viewed as an expert in your industry, is a key way of growing your social media following, building relationships and becoming key influencers within your industry.

5.7. Why You Should Have A Blog

Every business should have a blog. EVERY business. Yours is no different. And the best place for that blog to be? On your website. Yes, you can set up external blog sites, but why would you want your traffic to be sent anywhere other than your business site?

Blog posts give you great content for social media. We all want more web traffic; we wouldn't bother having websites if we didn't! Your website is where your potential customers go to find out more about you. It's a way for them to find you too. It's also somewhere that they can be directed to from social media. Although, why would someone click an update that read, 'find out more about us', 'get in touch with us', 'our clients', etc.? All worthwhile pages on your site, but not ones that are going to lead to huge traffic from social media.

That's where your blog comes in. Your blog is a great way of driving traffic to your website from social media. It gives you content for updates. It allows you to show your knowledge and position yourself as an expert. Google will love it too, as it provides regular fresh content and lots of lovely keywords! Of course, once people land on your blog post, they'll then be able to navigate round the rest of your site, and find out more about you. They'll be more 'bought in' to finding out about you, because you've just shared a pearl of wisdom with them!

So, that's why you should blog! The next question is...what should you blog about?!

5.8. What Should You Blog About?

So, now you know that you've got to have a blog on your site, it's time to start writing blog posts. What should you blog about? The first important step is to think about the person reading your blog posts. Who will they be? What can you give them that will deliver value to them? Knowledge is always a good place to start, as we all like to learn. It also helps position you as the experts. This type of blog post works much better than one purely focused on the business products and services, or client case studies.

I would aim to write a blog post every week. Some businesses produce them every day and, if you have the resource, it's a great strategy to have. But blog posts can be time consuming to create. If the resource is not available, once a week is much more achievable. Research suggests the ideal blog post length is around 1600 words. I'm a believer in not sticking to word limits. I've written longer blog posts, but most of mine are short and to the point. Typically, they are around the 500-word mark. They are quick to read, and they deliver value quickly too. Blogging for me is predominantly a way of positioning myself as an expert, while driving traffic to my site from social media. Both aims mean word count is not as important to me.

If you're stuck with what to blog about, here's a few ideas that might spark your thinking. Try to apply each of the ideas below to your own industry.

1. A list – e.g. 8 Ways to Reduce Cellulite
2. How to – e.g. How To Generate New Business With Direct Mail
3. A guide – e.g. A Guide to Managing Your Personal Finances
4. A comparison – e.g. Hootsuite or Buffer – A Comparison of Social Media Scheduling Tools
5. Day in the life – e.g. A Day In The Life of Our Business

6. A vlog (video blog) – e.g. Behind the Scenes At Our Latest Conference (VIDEO)
7. An interview – e.g. An Interview With Our Chief Executive
8. A gallery – e.g. Our Recent Charity Fancy Dress Day
9. A cheat sheet – e.g. Getting Your Business Goals Set in 10 Minutes
10. An infographic – e.g. Why Bees Are So Important To Our Survival
11. Mistakes made – e.g. 7 Mistakes Made By Businesses When Recruiting New Staff
12. Case Study – e.g. How One Of Our Clients Saved £10k in Tax, and You Can Too
13. Quick Tips – e.g. 52 Quick Tips for Getting a Six Pack
14. Q&A – e.g. Q&A of Questions We Received on Twitter
15. Latest thoughts – e.g. Our Thoughts On The Election Results and How It Could Affect You
16. Guest post – e.g. Guest Post From An Adwords Expert
17. A review – e.g. Our Thoughts On The Newest Gadget Everyone Wants
18. Your story – E.g. Our Company Story – How It All Began
19. Why – e.g. Why Most People Are Wrong About Their Diet Choices
20. An update – e.g. Where We've Been and What We've Been Up To

This is just a starter to get you thinking. You could just take one of these ideas and use none of the others; such as creating a weekly list. I find one of the easiest ways of generating blog post ideas is to brainstorm and come up with several at once. You may even find it easier to get a few written in one go, then you have them ready to go out over the coming weeks.

5.9. Sharing Your Blog Posts on Social Media

Once you have your blog posts written and published on your site, the next important step is to share them on social media.

The big mistake you can make with your blog posts is not sharing them often enough. After going to the effort of writing a blog post, one tweet just isn't enough. You should be sharing the blog post again, and again, and then again!

The number of times you share the post is platform specific. On Twitter, I would share a blog post at least 5 times. On Facebook and LinkedIn (both company page and personal profile), twice. You could also share an Instagram image relating to the post, and change the link in your profile temporarily to that of the blog post. Add the blog post to multiple Pinterest boards that the content relates to. The key is, don't make it difficult for people to find your post.

Scheduling is your friend when it comes to sharing your blog post! Use a scheduling tool, such as Hootsuite or Buffer, to schedule updates about your post (more on this later). On Twitter, I would share two updates that day about your post, then one a day over the next 3-4 days. You could even schedule more posts in the future, if your post is not time-specific. On Facebook and LinkedIn, I would share the post as soon as it has been published and again about 3 days later. The key is getting as many views on that blog post as possible. Remember, not all your followers and connections will be using those platforms at any one time. You are doing them a favour in making sure that they don't miss out on your post. You won't alienate those who read the post the first time you shared it, and are seeing future updates about it. It will hopefully just remind them how good the post was, and they may then share your update with their followers!

The key to sharing your blog post multiple times is to make sure each update is different. The first may simply take the structure of 'NEW

POST: *Post Title* [LINK]'. The next update might form a question about the post. You might create an update that highlights a point made in the post. You could check that they've seen the post, 'Did you see our recent post on *TITLE? [*LINK]'. Be sure to include an image with each update, as this will draw more attention to your post.

It is important to look at your Google Analytics to see what kind of traffic the blog post is receiving from social media. Use this to guide you as to your most popular blog posts, and the types of posts you can replicate again in the future.

5.10. Curating Content for Social Media

Being an expert in a field is more than just creating your own content to share. It also means finding good content on the web, and sharing it with your audience. It's about becoming the 'knowledge hub' for your audience. Yes, if they looked hard enough, they could find the information too, but you have done the hard-work for them, and they know they should follow you to get quick access to some great articles.

Curating good content can be just as important as creating good content. This means you need to find good content on the web, and then share it on social media. Content that you know will benefit your target audience, and that they will be interested in. It also means you get to read some great content and learn more yourself!

I worked with a large international technology firm and their sector managers on how they could be seen as thought leaders within their particular sectors. One of the focuses for this was finding great curated content, sharing it on LinkedIn and Twitter, and commenting on its content. This lead to the sector managers being seen as more influential within their sectors, landing them more PR opportunities and more customer interaction.

You can find great content in a variety of ways:

1. Twitter influencers

Create a list on Twitter of influencers in your industry. They are likely to share some great content that you could either retweet or share as a link within your own social media update.

2. Google 'Best Blogs/News Sites/Articles in the (NAME OF INDUSTRY) Industry'!

Google is your friend when it comes to finding good article sources. Google the above, adding in the necessary industry, and see what news and blog sites you find.

3. Set up Google Alerts

Google Alerts allows you to search keywords and be alerted either, every time your keyword is mentioned on the web, or, with a daily or weekly digest of keyword mentions.

4. Use Feedly

Once you've found (and keep finding) a list of good sites for articles, it can become a bit of a chore looking round them all for new articles. 'Feedly' is a great way of arranging these sites. You can set yourself up with an account online or on the app. Then create folders (e.g. social media, marketing, etc.) and add relevant sites by pasting in the link. Each time you go to your Feedly account, you will see which articles are new within your folders. I have Feedly set as my homepage, so that I can quickly see each day any new articles I want to read and share.

When sharing articles on social media, you could simply put the title of the article you're linking to, and the link. Or you could add your thoughts on it. Or maybe ask a question relating to the article, to encourage discussion.

5.11. Talking About Your Business on Social Media

We've already established the importance of not selling (too much). So, how can you talk about your business so that people know what you do without feeling like it's too salesy?

One of the simplest ways is to talk about what's happening that day. Not in an itemised diary, kind of way. Just bring your business to life by describing something you are doing that day for a customer. Let's look at a few examples:

1. A Clothes Shop
I'm looking at bringing in some new stock today to get ready for Spring!

2. An Accountant
It's been a great day here! We've just saved one of our clients £9,789 in tax.

3. A Personal Trainer
5am start to meet my first client. We're going to be focusing on weighted squats today.

4. A Leadership Development Company
Our team are working on a proposal today, to deliver some coaching to leaders in the chemical industry.

5. A Children's Nursery
Today our toddlers will be getting involved in some messy play with shaving foam!

You get the idea! Putting these out on social media occasionally, when there's something worth sharing in your day, is an excellent way of opening people's eyes to what you do. I know I've met many businesses before who, once they've described what their business is,

I'm still none the wiser! Yet if they describe something they've been working on for a client, I get it!

You'll see none of the above includes a sales message. There's no, 'if you want the same, give us a call on…'. It's just a statement about what's going on. Be sure to include an image too.

This also helps to speak to your target audience's subconscious. Our subconscious pays attention to things that are related to us. It's why you see pregnant women everywhere when you're expecting a baby, or every car on the road is a BMW when you're looking to buy one. If someone is having tax issues, and sees an update about tax saving, they're subconscious will zone in on it. The more detail you include - what, where, who, why, how - the more subconscious triggers you will hit.

5.12. Talking Non-Business on Social Media

There's an assumption for many businesses that they should be completely professional and corporate all the time. Of course, professionalism is key. I would never suggest you be discriminatory or a bully, for example, in your social media content.

The problem with focusing on professionalism and being corporate is that your social media loses the human touch. It doesn't encourage interaction and engagement. In short, it's not SOCIAL! If all we share on social media is business and industry-focused updates, we can quickly lose the social, personable, element. This can result in users being turned off from your activity, skipping over it, and potentially unfollowing you!

Adding in some more non-business-related content can really help to bring your social media activity to life. It encourages people to engage with you, it opens them up to the people within the business, and it keeps them interested in your content. I know, some of the best conversations I've had on social media, with those within my target market, have been sparked by talking about me and my life, and not about social media at all.

If you are a small business owner, you may give more of an idea of the person behind the business. What you get up to at the weekend. What your hobbies are. How many kids you have? Your morning stroll with Barney the dog! Whatever it is that you are comfortable and happy to share. I'm not saying that you should start using social media as your own personal diary, with pictures of your breakfast, telling people you're stopping for a coffee, and that you're so happy it's wine o'clock! You just share what works for you and your personality. I like the idea that people feel they 'know me' before they've even met me. The relationship is already on the way to being built, simply by giving a small glimpse into me and my life.

For larger organisations, this could be sharing what's going on in your office. Charity fancy dress day? Cake sale? Team night out? Someone running a marathon? The office football team being beaten yet again? A debate that's going around the office about the best biscuit for dunking? Again, do what works for your organisation and its culture.

Adding in these human elements really help your audience to build a relationship with your brand. The stronger the relationship, the more likely they are to buy.

5.13. Questions

Questions are so important in your social media content. I often get asked by my clients, 'how can we get more people replying to our posts?'. Well, why would someone reply if you give them nothing to reply to?! We reply to questions. Ask questions, and you will get more responses.

I know there is often the fear that you ask a question and no one replies. This does sometimes happen, but don't let it put you off. Even when someone reads a question, they are answering it in their head. You are 'opening up' their thinking and that's important too.
So, what questions should you ask?

It's great to ask questions that spark thinking in your audience that hopefully leads to you as the solution. For example, I once asked on Twitter – "Are you using Twitter lists for your business?". I got a lot of responses and had some great conversations around Twitter lists. One person, the Managing Director of an SME, responded that they didn't know lists existed! I helped her out, letting her know where she could find lists and how she could use them. She then asked me if I could deliver some training for them, as there was obviously lots of areas of social media they had not yet explored. I've since delivered three different training sessions for the same company. All from asking that simple question!
Brainstorm a list of questions you could ask on social media, based around your industry. You've then got a bank of questions you can use when you're stuck for content. It's also worth looking at every piece of content you put out on social media, and considering how you could end it with a question. For example, you could share your blog post link by asking a question raised or answered in the blog.

Even simple everyday questions often get good responses. "What are you all up to today?", "how's your day been?", "what's your drink of choice tonight?". Simple questions that get people chatting to you!

Questions can also be good for research. I often ask people to share which businesses they love to follow on social media, then I go and check those businesses out to see what they are doing right! Have a think of the questions you could ask of your audience that will give you knowledge you can use in your business.

If you are scheduling questions, make sure it's at a time when there is someone to handle the response. You don't want to be asking questions at 9am if you're not able to go on social media to handle responses until later that afternoon. Be open to the conversation. Remember, the more conversations you have with your target market, the more business you will get.

5.14. Lead Capture

Social media offers a great opportunity to capture leads. By a lead, I mean some details that allow you to get back in touch with the person. That could be an email address, a physical address, a phone number, a social media username, or any other means of future communication that allows you to market to that person going forward.

An easy lead to generate via social media is one giving a name (possible just a first name) and an email address. The cost to the person providing this information is limited. A lot of people feel protective of both their physical address and their phone number, but are happy to give their email address.

As a result, of them giving you their name and email address, you repay them with a benefit. Something free for them that will give them value. That could be:

- A free report
- A whitepaper
- A tutorial
- A video series
- A webinar
- A voucher
- A template

Or any other form of 'freebie' that you think will benefit them and lead them to give you their details.

You can send them to a page of your website that details the free 'thing' they will receive, and what's included within it, with a web form asking for their name and email address. Many email marketing service providers, such as Mailchimp, allow you to easily create these web forms and give you the code to add to your site. This will then link through to a specific list on that email system, and you can automate an email to go out with a link to their 'freebie'.

You could also try using what is called a squeeze page. A squeeze page is a single web page, that gives the content outlined above. But they are unable to navigate elsewhere. Hosting the page on your website as normal will allow them to click away to other areas of your site. On a squeeze page, they have only two options – fill in the form or leave the site. This often leads to a higher volume of people completing the form, as they are not distracted by other pages on the site. You could still link them through to your normal site when they have completed the form, to generate that traffic and encourage them to learn more about you, but you have the lead, which is the most important thing at this stage.

For example, I have a document that I give away for free – 50 Content Ideas for Social Media. On the various social media platforms, I regularly post updates along the following lines: "Stuck for social media content, and never know what to say? Download my list of 50 content ideas for social media [LINK]". The link takes users through to a squeeze page giving a bit more information about what they'll get from the list, and a web form for them to complete, which links through to my CRM system. Within minutes of completing the form, they have the document in their inbox. On completing the form, they are redirected through to my site. And I have new leads for my business! I sell, the majority of, my workshops and online courses via email marketing, so this is an ideal way for me to generate new business through social media!

The more information you ask for from your leads, the more you need to give them in return, as there is a bigger 'cost' to them. For example, if you need physical addresses, then you need to have a physical product to send them in the post that they would really want. I loved Graze's campaign where they delivered a free Graze box to you. The cost to the consumer was their name, email address, phone number, address, and even credit card details. They received their free box of goodies, but had to be sure to cancel before a certain date to ensure that they received no more boxes. I'm sure many either forgot or loved their box enough that they decided to start paying for them. It was a very clever campaign, and one that they used social media heavily for.

So, start thinking about the perfect lead capture that you could share on social media. What would incite your audience to click the link and then give you their details? What is the best thing you can offer to them that will pull them in as a lead?

5.15. Offers

Offers are a great way to sell on social media. The work you have done with the posts that don't promote anything, but are there to build relationships, will pay off when you release offers via social media. Offers could include money off, or additional products, or services on top of those that they have purchased. They should be exciting to your audience and make them want to buy straight away. 10% off doesn't really do it for anyone any more. It's not going to make them take notice and buy straight away. On the flip side, don't offer a huge discount, as this may reduce credibility for your product or service.

Your offers should also be deadlined. There is no urgency to buy if the offer is ongoing. A deadline also gives a countdown to talk about that offer on social media. 2 days left, 1 day left, an hour left, etc. Quick flash offers can work very well, when it is only available on that day, or for a few days.

You could release your offers with videos and imagery to support that offer. Be sure to share it several times on each platform in the run up to the deadline. On Facebook, you can choose the 'create an offer' option on your page. This runs the offer through Facebook, sending the offer directly to the Facebook user. It is also worthwhile advertising your offer to get it in front of a larger audience (see the advertising section for more on this).

5.16. Running Competitions on Social Media

Competitions are a great way of increasing engagement and your following. This can lead to higher reach and an increased brand awareness. And, hopefully, an increase in new and returning customers! The prize doesn't have to be of great cost. In fact, it's been found that people are more likely to enter competitions with lower cost prizes as they feel they have a greater chance of winning!

Each platform has their own guidelines, so be sure to check these out before running a competition. Most are relaxed around the use of competitions. Facebook does have some stricter competition guidelines that you will need to be aware of. You cannot ask people to share your competition on their own or a friend's timeline. You cannot ask people to tag their friends in the comments of the post. If you breech Facebook's competition guidelines, Facebook will ask you to remove the competition post. If you regularly breech them, your page may be removed from Facebook. Be sure to check competition guidelines, as they are changed regularly.

A few approaches you could take to a competition include:

1. Get entrants to comment on a post
You can ask for comments on a post in return for an entry to a competition. You could simply state that all comments will be entered in to a draw to win the prize, and ask them to answer a simple question, caption an image, or fill in a blank. Or you could ask them to answer a question correctly in the comments and do a draw from those who are correct. This works best on both Facebook and Instagram.

2. Get entrants to like a post
You could also ask people to like a post (you could do this as well as asking them to comment to really boost engagement). Again, you then enter all those who like the post into a draw.

3. Get entrants to add a picture

You can ask people to add a picture in the comments section on Facebook. Or you could ask them to post a photo on Instagram or Twitter, tagging the business username in their post, and using a specific hashtag. For example, a restaurant could ask customers to post a picture of their food whilst dining at the restaurant on Instagram, tagging the restaurant in it, to be entered in to a draw to win a meal for two.

4. Get entrants to share a post

As mentioned above, you can't do this on Facebook. But you can on the other platforms. Instagram can be trickier, as you need a separate app to share Instagram images, but it's easy to ask people to retweet an update on Twitter.

5. Get entrants to follow you on a platform

You can ask people to follow you on Instagram, or Twitter, to be entered in to a draw. This usually works better in combination with another request (e.g. retweet and follow us to be entered in to our draw).

6. Get entrants to give you their details

Rather than running the competition directly on social media and using it to increase engagement and following, you could direct people to a web page asking for their name and email address (or other details you may require) to enter the competition. This can be an excellent way of increasing leads to market too.

Be sure that the prize you are offering is one that is most relevant to your target audience. Even better if it aligns with your business, such as a free product or service. There are many people who will trawl social media for competitions. Having a generic prize may get you more entries, but may mean you give it away to someone who will never be a potential customer. Monthly competitions of small prizes work very well, and you can even run them continuously (such as in the example of the restaurant food picture above), drawing a winner at the end of each month.

To select your winner, there are several tools available, such as 'Woobox'. To notify the winner, you can either comment on the competition post, run another post stating who the winner is (and tagging them if possible), directly messaging that entrant where possible, or by emailing them if you have collected their email address.

5.17. Video

Video is a great content format for social media. Most businesses are put off creating video content because they believe that it requires a full scale expensive production, but the majority of businesses will have multiple means of quickly recording video content. Smartphones and tablets can produce a video to be uploaded in a matter of seconds. They create authentic video content too; content that the audience is more likely to engage with than videos that feel like a slick advert.

Video is an excellent way of introducing the people within your business, of bringing your business to life, of sharing knowledge, of engaging with your audience, of showing your brandonality, of bringing people to events with you, of conducting interviews, and much, much, more! These videos can form content for your YouTube channel, as well as being shared directly to other platforms like Facebook and Twitter.

Vlogging is becoming ever more popular. A vlog is, essentially, a video blog. The content can take the same kind of format as your written blog posts. You can deliver the content directly to the camera, take the camera on a journey with you and create a 'day in the life' video, or showcase an event, or you could capture the screen and share slides, or a tutorial for doing something online.

When creating videos, some editing is likely to be needed, unless you can create one-take videos. You will still probably need to chop out the beginning and end. Most computers come with free editing equipment. Windows has MovieMaker, while Macs have iMovie. Both are easy to use and allow you to do basic editing techniques.

To record your screen, you can use Jing for free. Camtasia is a higher level option, with the ability to zoom in and out, and great editing features. For capturing video, you can simply use your smartphone or tablet. Or invest in a camera. I love my Canon G7x for filming vlogs, as it is lightweight, compact and has a flip screen so you can see yourself in the shot. It also takes good quality videos too.

Most people will watch videos without audio. This means subtitles are essential in improving your viewer figures. I use an app called Clips to quickly create videos on my smartphone. I share short videos with a social media tip, and Clips adds the subtitles as I'm speaking. I edit any mistakes it has made and load the video up to Facebook, Instagram and Twitter. The whole process takes me 5 minutes maximum. The result has been incredible! I was invited to speak at an event in South Africa solely as a result of the company seeing my short videos.

The key is to just hit that record button! The slightly imperfect but authentic video that gets uploaded will always deliver better than the perfect slick advert-quality video that doesn't!

5.18. Go Live

With the sheer volume of social media use, it's clear we need to do something different to stand out. We've got to be prepared to do what other businesses won't.
And that is why going live on social media can have such a positive impact. IF you get it right!

Most businesses won't go live. It's too scary. Something might go wrong: so they don't. They stay in their safe social media bubble of posting sales updates and business broadcasts. A bubble that doesn't really let their audience in.

Going live on social media helps pull your audience in. It builds authenticity. Yes, something could go wrong, and that's what makes it real, compared to a full-scale video recorded and edited by a videographer. It's what makes people want to watch, and it really helps to build relationships with your audience.

You can go live on your Facebook Page, Facebook Groups and Facebook Events, as well as your personal profile. Facebook live videos get much higher reach than most forms of content on your page. Your audience will be bigger AND they'll be more engaged. To go live on Twitter, you can use their standalone app Periscope and you can go live on Instagram too.

On both Twitter and Facebook, your live video goes directly on to your profile and can be viewed after the live event. On Instagram, the live video is not saved anywhere and cannot be viewed after the broadcast.

Make sure you plan your live event. Think through what you want to achieve and what you want to get across to your audience. Plan the time and date that you will go live. Make clear notes on what you want to include in the live broadcast. Learn them, but also have them somewhere in sight to give you confidence that you cover all you want to. Tell your audience that you will be going live. Give them notice, on social media and your other marketing channels.

Your live broadcast could include:

- A behind the scenes look at your business
- An interview with an industry expert, or someone within your business
- A Q&A, encouraging viewers to ask questions in the comments
- An introduction of a new product or service
- A live broadcast of an event

And many, many, others.

I have recently spoken at numerous events for local council clerks. One attendee shared that their local council meetings were attracting around three people to attend. They decided to broadcast the meeting live on Facebook, and they had 2000 people view the live meeting! They were also able to comment and send in their questions to be covered in the meeting. It was a great success for the council and something they are going to continue to do.

The more live broadcasts you do, the easier they will come to you. The key is to get that first one in the bag! Plan it, practice it and then do it. And learn from it. Live isn't meant to be perfect, so don't worry if it isn't. The more you do, the more confident you will become in doing them.

5.19. Using Hashtags

A hashtag is the # symbol followed by letters or numbers, without the use of any punctuation (no spaces, full stops, commas, apostrophes – a grammar lover's nightmare!). When posted within an update, this creates a clickable link to other mentions of that hashtag on that platform. As such, all updates around a topic on a platform can be brought in to the same stream. Most social media platforms do now support the use of hashtags.

Using hashtags within your posts will increase their reach to audiences looking for that hashtag. It can also help to increase your followers, as you become visible to a wider audience. Be sure to only include hashtags that are relevant to your post and don't add them for the sake of it. Ask yourself whether the hashtag is going to lead the right audience to you.

If you are targeting people in your local area, using local hashtags can be a good way to increase visibility locally. Look at what hashtags influencers within your industry are using to find industry specific hashtags. There are many tools on the web, such as hashtagify.me, which will help you find the right hashtags to use.

Hashtags can be quite off-putting when used within updates. Our brains don't read them as easily as normal words. As such, updates with hashtags within them can often be scrolled over rather than read. I would recommend using your hashtags at the end of your update so that you don't confuse the message. On Instagram, you should use as many hashtags as possible to get your content found. If you include your hashtags within the comments of your post, rather than the post itself, it separates them from the post, while still allowing it to be found, and you can send your post to Facebook without a long list of hashtags appearing with it.

You can search for hashtags used by others within the search bar on each platform.

5.20. Using Your Own Hashtags

There are updates in which it is worth using your own hashtag. What do I mean 'your own'? Essentially, a hashtag that you have created that no one else is using. To create your own hashtag, think of one that is relevant to what you want to use it for (e.g. #samflynntips), then run a search for it on that platform. If the search returns that there are no results, then go ahead and use that hashtag.

You don't have to apply to use a hashtag and you don't own the use of that hashtag. Anyone can use it whether it is in the right context or not. Having your own hashtag will allow you to link together posts of a similar nature.

This can be good for:

- Daily/weekly tips (e.g. #samflynntips)
- Events (e.g. #SamsSuccessEvent)
- Competitions (e.g. #winwithsamflynn)
- Offers (e.g. #savewithsamflynn)
- Facts (e.g. #samsfacts)
- Thoughts (e.g. #fromthemindofsamflynn)
- Q & As (e.g. #asksamflynn)
- Linking tweets around a topic (e.g. #SamTalksLinkedIn)

Be sure to use the hashtag you create regularly, and monitor use of it to ensure you know when someone is trying to engage with the hashtag by running searches for it on that platform or using a tool like www.socialmention.com to receive alerts when the hashtag is used.

5.21. The Reach Issue

Facebook and Instagram are both such great platforms to market your business on. Mainly because of the volume of use! But there is a big issue for businesses when it comes to marketing on these platforms – REACH!

The reach of each of your posts is how many times that post has appeared in user's timelines. So, if your reach is 386, then the post has appeared in 386 timelines. This doesn't translate directly as people who have read your post. Purely that it appeared in their timeline. If they skipped over it, it still counts as reach.

Back when Facebook pages for businesses first came in to existence, it was as simple as everyone liking your page seeing your updates in the timeline. But as Facebook has grown bigger and bigger, and people are adding more and more friends, and more and more pages that they like, Facebook have realised that they can no longer show everything from every friend and every page in your timeline, or you'll very quickly grow to hate Facebook and leave. So, for the longevity of the platform, they had to come up with an alternate solution.

Facebook's main aim is to give users what they would like to see, and to ensure they keep coming back to Facebook. Bearing this in mind, the predominant determinant of reach is how engaged they are with your content. When a user first likes your page, their engagement is classed as being as high as it can possibly be. So, Facebook delivers the content of the page to that user. If, after they've seen a few updates from the page, and they haven't engaged in any way (liked, commented, watched, clicked, shared), then Facebook will decide that the user isn't really that interested in the page and will stop showing the content of the page in that user's timeline.

Similarly, Facebook has a sneaky way of knowing what you are interested in. When you are logged in to the app on your phone, for example, Facebook can determine your interests by what you are browsing on the internet on your phone. It is more likely to show you a page's posts if the page falls in your interests (e.g. food, clothes shopping, etc.). For example, I liked the Facebook page of a shop that sells wool (I crochet as a stress reliever!!). I hadn't seen any of their updates in ages. Then I bought some wool from that shop and within an hour, I was seeing their updates again!

Facebook is also more likely to show content that has proven popular with others, especially your Facebook friends. If lots of people are engaging with an update, then Facebook would assume that more people will be interested in it, and the organic reach will keep going up. Sharing certainly has a huge impact, as it leads to that content appearing in far more timelines.

As Instagram is owned by Facebook, the same issue is now present on Instagram. So, increasing reach on both platforms should definitely be one of your social media aims.

5.22. Increasing Reach

Reach can be increased organically (i.e. without paying for advertising) in a variety of ways.

1. Use more video

Facebook gives higher reach to video. Share video content and you'll see your reach increase compared to that of other posts. This is particularly true of native video (i.e. video that has been uploaded directly to Facebook, rather than shared as a link to another video hosting site like YouTube).

2. Ask questions

You need your audience to engage with your posts to ensure they see future posts, and that Facebook classes them as being interested in your page's content. So, encourage them to comment by giving them a reason to! Ask questions rather than posting statements. Aim to end each update with a question. You could even ask them to leave the answer in the comments.

3. Give a call to action

Make sure your update has some form of call to action for them to engage. For example, tell them to click the link to find out more. Or ask them to click like if they agree. Or get them to post a related picture in the comments. Or get them to tag a friend who the update is relevant to in the comments. People are more likely to engage if you tell them to!

4. Go live

Live video is given even more reach than non-live video! Go live and again you'll see the reach increase!

5. Run competitions

Competitions are a great way of incentivising engagement. Ask a question that they must respond to too be entered in to a prize draw. In Facebook's competition guidelines, you are not allowed to incentivise shares, so you cannot ask your audience to share a post to have a chance of winning a prize.

6. Post regularly

Don't just come on to your Facebook page when you've something to say. Try to get something on their every day to allow your audience to build a relationship with your brand and content.

7. Know what your audience wants

Understand your audience inside and out. Survey them to understand what content they would be most interested in. Use your Facebook insights to see what content they are most engaged with, and replicate this. Stop posting content that you know they won't be interested in.

5.23. Scheduling Your Content

Social media doesn't have to be an 'in the moment' activity. There are lots of great tools available that allow you to preschedule your social media updates. This should make it far easier to allow time for social media. I know I could easily get through a busy work day without posting anything on social media. Plus, there are the days I take off with my girls, when I don't want to be stuck to my phone or laptop, but still want to have an online presence. That's where scheduling makes things far easier!

There are lots of forms of content that can easily be scheduled:

- Blog posts
- Articles
- Tips
- Infographics
- Offers
- Images
- Videos
- Questions
- Competitions
- Campaigns

And much more!!!!

I wouldn't recommend scheduling too far in advance. It's useful to be on the ball with what's going out every day. And you could end up with a big editing job if you schedule months in advance and then things change within the business, or the outside world. I like to schedule weekly, as that is what works best for me. But you could certainly plan and schedule a full campaign, from beginning to end.

Scheduling doesn't mean you should never post live. I think it's important to do a mix, as it can be obvious when all activity is scheduled. It can lead your audience to see your accounts as more computerised and less human, so make sure you add some live elements in too. Take images that capture that moment, and talk about what's happening. Or share something that's just happened. Keep it real and authentic, while still making it as manageable as possible for you.

Be sure that you are aware every day of what is scheduled to go out. If it leads to engagement, you still need to be able to manage the response. So, don't ask questions if you know you're going to have very little access to social media all day, as you don't want to open-up conversation when you're unavailable to answer.

I really like Buffer (www.buffer.com) for scheduling social media content. Buffer allows you to set up a regular schedule for your updates to go out on each platform. For example, you might pick four times, across the day, that you would like content to be posted to Twitter. You then add content to your Buffer queue, and Buffer will release it at those times. You can also choose a set scheduled time, or share straight away, or add to the top of your queue. The thing that I love most about Buffer, is the browser extension. This means, when I'm reading a great social media article, I can just click the Buffer button on my browser, and add the article straight to my Buffer queue. It's a simple to use tool, and I would recommend checking it out.

If you prefer to do more than just schedule content, then have a look at Hootsuite. Hootsuite will allow you to set a time for your content to go out. But you are also able to see more on Hootsuite. You can see feeds for the platforms you add to it and you can create streams that allow you to easily see your mentions and comments. There's a lot more functionality than Buffer in terms of fully managing your social media activity.

There are several scheduling tools available beyond Buffer and Hootsuite, such as Tweetdeck, Sprout Social and Sprinklr, so have a look at them all to get a feel for which would work best for you.

Whatever tool you choose to use, I would consider scheduling your social media content to help you plan what is going out and when!

5.24. CASE STUDY – THE BODY COACH

Joe Wicks, otherwise known as The Body Coach, is someone who has built his whole business on the back of his social media activity. Joe is a great example of using his brandonality. In other words, being himself and letting his personality come across on social media. He doesn't pretend to be anyone he isn't and is now known for his catch phrases and jovial, outgoing approach.

Joe was a self-employed personal trainer in London. He decided to try something different with his Instagram account and started sharing videos of quick healthy recipes. He created the hashtag #LeanIn15 for the videos, as Instagram videos were a max of 15 seconds long at the time and the recipes were those that could be made within 15 minutes. Joe's following quickly grew; to the point where he landed himself a book deal, and has just released his 4th bestseller at the time of writing.

Joe continues to create great content for social media that appeals to his audience. He's stuck to what he is known for – sharing recipe and workout videos. He has a huge following on Instagram, Facebook, Twitter, Snapchat and YouTube. His media use varies. He posts his #LeanIn15 videos, images, blog posts, and goes live regularly as well, with live workouts and cook-a-longs. He also utilises Instagram stories and Snapchat to share what he is up to through his day.

He encourages engagement, asking people to 'double tap' (like on Instagram) if the recipe is 'a bit of them' or to tag someone who might want to try it. He also runs regular competitions to win copies of his books and DVD.

Plus, he gives us a bit of an insight in to his life, sharing holiday pictures and pictures of his cute nephew! He's a great example of someone who has used social media to increase his personal brand, which has ultimately lead to his business expanding. He now has a HQ in London with a growing team, selling not only his renowned books, but also his DVD and online fat loss programme.

As a great example of someone who has expanded their business mainly through their social media content, and has stuck to what works best for his audience, then Joe is your go to!

5.25. SUMMARY

- Your content is the most important part of your activity
- You need to consider the personality of your brand (brandonality) and what your audience want from you
- Don't sell too much
- Share your best knowledge, your own blogs and other people's content
- Use hashtags, images, videos and live streams
- Ask questions and take the opportunity to capture leads with your content
- Talk about your business, and things that are not related to your business
- Run deadlined offers and competitions
- Use video, go live, know your audience and encourage engagement to increase reach

WANT MORE?

There is a download over at www.samflynn.co.uk/bookresources giving you 50 content ideas for social media!

CHAPTER 6

ENGAGEMENT AND BUILDING RELATIONSHIPS

6.1. Engagement

Engagement has been a social media buzz word pretty much since social media became a 'thing' for businesses and the term isn't going anywhere! That's because it is so important! Businesses often have a habit of forgetting the SOCIAL in social media. They focus on the platforms as being a means of getting their message out to the world. A form of media, and it absolutely is.

But, if you neglect the *social* in social media you won't see anywhere near as much success with it. Social suggests interaction. It suggests people talking to one another, not just one person talking to a crowd. It suggests questions and responses. It suggests listening and responding to others as much as people responding to you.

Engaging and being social is a vital step for businesses as it can be very difficult to form relationships without being social. Imagine going on a first date, and the potential future love of your life talks non-stop about themselves, talks over you when you try to talk, and doesn't ask you a single question. Chances are you won't be taking it to a second date! Relationships can be very difficult to get off the ground without two-way conversation.
The way I view it is, the more conversations I have with my target market, the more business I get. Why wouldn't I want to encourage conversation?

Engagement essentially implies that you have taken an action with some content, or someone has taken an action with yours. It might be a share or retweet, a like, a mention, a reply, a video view or a click. Whatever action it takes, you need to encourage it to take place. Be open to engagement on social media and let those customer relationships flourish!

6.2. Building Relationships

If there's one thing that is important in business, it's relationship, and this includes the relationship between the business and both the current customer and the potential customer. Customers are more likely to become loyal, and buy from you again and again, IF they have built up a relationship with your business. Indeed, potential customers are more likely to start buying from you if a relationship has been formed.

Social media is a great way to build those relationships. It allows us to get 1 on 1 with our customers and deliver extra value to them. It allows them to see if we are the type of business they'd like to work with. It allows us to answer their questions quickly, and gives them an easy means of getting in touch with us.

Relationships are vital in building a loyal customer base. One of the best things about loyal customers is not just that they keep buying from you, but also that they talk to people they know too! They spread the word for you, including on social media. They are more likely to share your updates, give you glowing reviews, and advise other people to use your product or service when they are requesting recommendations.

Don't just use social media as a form of broadcasting your message. Use it to build relationships. As that is how social media converts into paying customers and business growth.

6.3. Increasing Engagement

We are all looking for engagement when it comes to social media, and yet it can be very difficult to achieve. How can we encourage someone to stop and take an action, rather than just reading our content or scrolling straight past it?

1. Get Your Content Right
We've already covered this in the content section. Make sure your content stands out and that it is relevant to your audience.

2. Ask Them To Respond
Why would people respond if you haven't asked them to? You could ask questions, ask them to fill in the gap (e.g. The best thing about my day was_____), ask them to caption an image, ask them to tag a friend, ask them to click like if they agree...whatever action you want them to take, ask them to take it!

3. Post Videos
A watch of a video is classed as engagement on social media. Post more video content and monitor your views to see which videos work best for your audience.

4. Use Your Insights
There'll be more of this in the measurement section, but insights are super important in understanding what works for your audience. Look at which updates get the highest engagement, and which get the lowest. Use that information to guide what works for your audience.

5. Engage Back
Don't encourage response and then ignore it. If someone comments or replies, be sure to respond back.

6. Post Regularly

It's hard for people to build a relationship with you unless you post regularly.

6.4. Getting Shares and Retweets

Shares and retweets are extremely valuable on social media. They not only get you in front of more people, but they also provide a peer review that someone agrees with your update. As such, those who are friends or followers of the person doing the sharing are more likely to be interested in that update. It brings in new followers too and, potentially, new customers.

Sharing updates is available on most platforms. On Facebook, both pages and people can share updates. On Twitter, users can hit the retweet button and either send the update out as it is or add their own thoughts to it as well. On LinkedIn, you can share both personal and company page updates. On Pinterest, you can re-pin a pin to your own board. Instagram is a little different, as you need an app allowing you to post re-grams. But the option is still there.

So, how can you get more shares and retweets?

The key is understanding what will appeal to your target audience. Your audience is more likely to click share or retweet if they agree with your content, are engaged by it, enjoy it, or get value from it. So, your first step is to highlight who your target audience is, and then understand what content appeals to them.

A few things that will certainly help you get retweets and shares are:

- Use of images
- Use of video
- Knowledge sharing
- Tips
- Humour
- Valuable links

Use your insights and analytics on each platform too, to see which content received the most retweets and shares. Make sure you replicate that kind of content moving forward.

6.5. Increasing Customer Loyalty

Social media can offer a great way of increasing the loyalty of your customers. Loyal customers aren't just satisfied. They are so loyal to your brand that they wouldn't consider going elsewhere. They will return to your business and buy repeatedly from it. They will become a lifetime customer and they will spend more with you during that lifetime.

It is, after all, far easier to sell to people we've already sold to than to try and bring in new customers. So long as you have delivered a great, product, or service, they know what you can do. You don't have to convince them like you do with new customers. So, encouraging their loyalty can often be a more successful marketing strategy than trying to bring in new customers. They will also shout out about you, meaning they do the marketing for you!

So, what role can social media play in increasing customer loyalty?

Well firstly, it means they won't quickly forget about you. You need to encourage your customers to like and follow you on social media, so that they see your updates, and are reminded of the great product/service you gave them. You need to make sure your content is interesting and valuable to them so that they maintain their interest in you and do so in a positive way.

Secondly, they can grow their relationship with you. By engaging with you on social media, and by you responding to their updates, their relationship with your brand grows. You can respond to their updates, on platforms like Twitter and LinkedIn, even if they are not mentioning your business. They will feel special that you are paying attention to them.

Thirdly, you could wow them. If you see an opportunity to deliver a wow, take it! It could be that they mention it's their birthday, so you fire a card in the post or a small gift. They might be announcing a success, and you send flowers. It won't always be possible, but look out for those opportunities when you can really wow them. We all love surprises and will often post on social media when we receive them. So, look for opportunities on social media to surprise your customers.

Increasing customer loyalty and the lifetime value of your customers is a great way to grow your business. Social media is a brilliant tool to help do it!

6.6. Twitter Lists

The users you follow on Twitter are probably a mixed bag. There might be your current customers in there, your potential customers, people you know, other businesses you're interested in, and all the other different Twitter users you end up following during your Twitter lifetime.

As a result, it can make your timeline a big jumble of updates from everyone that you follow. You might want to engage with your current customers, for example, and respond to their tweets, but you need to sift through all the other content before you find them, if you manage to find them at all.

That's why Twitter lists are so useful!

Twitter lists allow you to add users to a list. Then when you go to that list, you will see the updates of all users in the list only. For example, you could create a list of your customers on Twitter. You then click on your customers list and see the updates of your customers. You can then work your way through engaging with your customers and responding to things they are saying. You build the relationship you have already formed with them and increase their loyalty as a result.

You can have as many lists as you want on Twitter and you have the option to make the lists either public or private. If you select for your list to be public, users will be notified when they have been added to the list. Anyone can go to your profile and look at your public lists and who is on them. Probably not the best approach if you don't want to reveal who your customers are! Making your list private means that the user is not aware they are on the list and no one else can find the list. It is for your use only.

Lists do not affect how you send out tweets. You cannot send a tweet to a list. They just allow you to see the updates of the users you wish to see the updates of more clearly.

Lists you might create include:

- Customers
- Potential customers (you could even split this down into categories, if you have different target markets)
- Local businesses
- Industry influencers
- Sources of good content
- Referrers
- Event attendees
- Celebrities
- Friends

And any others you wish to create! They are for your use, so create them to make it as easy as possible to see the updates of the users you wish to.

6.7. Sending Messages To Your LinkedIn Connections

You've worked hard to build up your connections on LinkedIn. And then what? They just sit there in the background adding little or no benefit to your business? I have had so many conversations with businesses who are surprised they have had little or no new business through LinkedIn, as they have such a high number of connections. Just having connections is unlikely to bring you lots of business. Communicating and building a relationship with them will.

One of the great things about being connected to someone on LinkedIn is that you don't need their email address to communicate with them. You can do it directly through LinkedIn via messaging. Messaging allows you to send messages to those you are connected to. It's a great way to communicate, as they likely to pay a bit more attention to a LinkedIn message coming in to their inbox, which is also sitting in their LinkedIn inbox, than yet another salesy email.

The important thing with LinkedIn messaging is to not abuse it. Don't use the opportunity as a means of spamming your connections. Instead use it as an opportunity to build the relationship. When you first connect with them, take some time to read through their profile and maybe read a post that they have published. If there's some opportunity within their profile, or their post, to send them a message and start a conversation, then take that opportunity. "Good to connect with you! I see you used to work at XYZ. Do you know Dave Jones? I used to deal with him there a lot". Or, "It's great to connect on here with you. Just had a read of your latest post. I really like the point you make about.....". There's no selling going on. You're not doing what a lot of people do when they first connect, which reads a little something like this..."Thanks for connecting. Let me introduce you to my business. We have x number of years' experience in delivering....blah...blah...blah"! It doesn't work!!!

The messaging opportunity should really be seen as a means by which to build the relationship. To take those first steps into a long term working relationship. To build the rapport. You may then send them an article you've written that you thought may be of interest to them. Or, invite them to download your lead capture, as you think the information within it could be really valuable to them. Only when you've had a few interactions would it be ok to ask them to meet up or chat over the phone. Relationships are much easier to build if they warm up gradually, rather than trying to jump straight in while the relationship is still cold.

Don't abuse the messaging feature; use it to build relationships, and it can be a very powerful way of generating a lot of business through LinkedIn. Don't be afraid to occasionally share offers or events you have going on. I often fill at least one place at each of my workshops by finding connections I think would be interested in my workshops, and then letting them know about them via messaging. Each time, I have lots of response from people apologising that they can't make it but to please keep them informed about future workshops.

Start planning the messages you could send on LinkedIn and the sequence you could work through to build the relationship and get the meeting!

6.8. Dealing with Negativity and Complaints

The rise of social media offers a huge opportunity for businesses, but there are downsides too. Where customers would previously make complaints directly to businesses, away from the public eye, they now often take to social media to raise their grievances. The result is that the complaint no longer exists solely between the customer and the business. It is there for all to see.

I've heard many businesses state their reason for not using social media is because they don't want to encourage negative customer response and damage their reputation. The problem is, a customer can tarnish your reputation via social media whether you're using it or not. In fact, it's much less likely to be damaged if you are there to handle the response rather than ignore it and allow it to escalate.

The easiest way to manage customer negativity and complaints on social media? Avoid them altogether! We are in an age now where poor customer service cannot be accepted from businesses. The more customers who go online to complain, the bigger the damage to the business. So, the easiest step to eliminate customer complaints is to never give them a reason to complain! There are businesses out there who don't spend any money on marketing. Instead, they deliver an exceptional customer service and always go beyond the customer's expectations. As such, their customers do the marketing for them, and they instead spend money pleasing their customers. It's a great strategy to have, as their customers will be shouting their praises all over social media, and bringing in new customers, who will then do the same, and the cycle continues!

But of course, we all drop the ball now and again. So, it is important to have a strategy in place for managing complaints on social media. The crucial first step is to neither ignore nor delete the complaint. You MUST handle it. I've heard of a business whose reputation was massively damaged when they deleted a customer complaint from their Facebook page. The customer then sent a message to all their friends to post complaints, and they were left with over 70 complaints on their page instead of one!

It is important that you respond appropriately to the complaint. Firstly, never enter in to an argument. Remember, you are not just responding to that customer. You are being watched by your other customers and potential customers too. Arguments can quickly escalate online. So, even if you know the customer is in the wrong, don't tell them they are! The best approach is to take the conversation offline. If you have their details, tell them you will give them a call. If you haven't, ask them to send you a private message with their details and you'll get in touch. Be empathetic in your response and state how upset you are to hear that things did not go as planned for the customer.

Once you have handled the complaint offline, go back online and state that it was great to talk to them and you are glad the issue has been resolved. This is for the other eyes that are watching the complaint unfurl, showing that you have managed it and not ignored it.
There will be situations when you will have to delete complaints (where possible. You cannot delete a negative mention on Twitter for example). If bad language is used, your customers would rather the complaint was removed than you leave it there while you are handling it. On your Facebook page, you can set up a profanity filter in the settings so that no one is able to post profanities on your page.

If you are receiving unfounded negativity, often referred to as trolling, where it is not a complaining customer, but someone set on bringing the business down, you can, of course, report this to the platform in question, and block the user. This is a different scenario, and your customers will usually be 'on your side', as it is not a regular customer complaint.

Spread positivity on social media, and deliver an exceptional level of customer service, and hopefully you will never be in the situation of managing negativity. But be ready just in case!

6.9. CASE STUDY – SAINSBURY'S

Sainsbury's deliver a great customer service on all the social media platforms they are present on. They answer all customer queries quickly and with a very friendly tone. One thing that really stands out in the way Sainsbury's interact with their customers via social media, is the sign off on each response. Whoever has answered the query or responded to the comment will sign off with their name. This is a great way to personalise your social media engagement approach. Most people would rather speak to a person than a machine, and knowing the name of that person makes the process feel much friendlier and engaging.

Sainsbury's also handle complaints effectively on social media. Even when complaints are made about non-Sainsbury's products bought in store, Sainsbury's still respond and suggest contacting the company, while also offering a refund for the product or a Sainsbury's gift card. They see the value in keeping customers happy on social media, and it pays off.

Sainsbury's know what works for their audience on social media, and deliver it. They add humorous posts, recipes and food inspiration, as well as occasionally sharing what is new or on offer in store. They get lots of engagement as a result, with hundreds of likes, shares and comments on each post.

They also respond with humour. If you've not heard of the infamous 'fishy' exchange that Sainsbury's had with a customer on Twitter, then you should certainly look it up. The conversation continued for three hours, with both the customer and the Sainsbury's customer service team coming up with fish-related pun after pun!

So, how could you use some of Sainsbury's approaches in your business? Firstly, response, and speed of response is important. If you don't have the resource in place to manage response, consider how you could do this to get the most from your social media activity. Secondly, be personable. The more personable you are in your approach, the more positive the outcome generally is. Finally, know your audience; know what works for them, and what they engage with, and give them it!

6.10. SUMMARY

- Engagement on social media is important for building relationships with your audience and increasing reach
- To increase engagement, ask for it, know what works for your audience, post regularly, include video posts and engage back
- To get more shares and retweets, understand what motivates your audience and what they relate most to
- Engaging with your current customers is great for increasing customer loyalty
- Twitter lists make it easier to engage with key people on Twitter
- Send regular messages to your LinkedIn connections
- Have a plan in place for how you will deal with negativity and complaints. Always respond.

WANT MORE?

Download 20 Ways To Increase Engagement over at www.samflynn.co.uk/bookresources.

CHAPTER 7

MEASUREMENT

7.1. Measuring Your Social Media Activity

It's very important that you measure your social media activity. Without measuring the results, it is very difficult to determine whether it's working or not, and whether you are using the right or wrong approach. Measuring also gives you a means by which to report your activity to anyone who needs the information. It can help to form an idea of return on investment (ROI), and how much business is being generated from your activity. We also talked about setting aims for your activity. You need to ensure that you are measuring whether these aims are being met.

There are several measures which would suggest 'success' of your activity if they are growing. They are also good measures of brand awareness, as more people will become aware of your brand, as a result of each of these measures. They are:

- Increase in followers/connections/likes
- Increase in mentions
- Increase in engagement – comments, likes, shares, clicks
- Increase in post reach

If you aimed to get more web traffic, then you need to look at how many visits are coming directly from social media to your website.

If you are aiming to increase sales with your social media activity, then you specifically need to look at how many sales are being made as a result of the activity. This can be a difficult one. Particularly if you don't sell online. For example, someone might have been following your company on social media for a while, engaged with you, and really built up a good relationship. They then decide to take the next step, go to look at your website, and give you a ring to arrange a meeting. At some point in the sales process you may ask them how they found out about your company, and they could state that they've heard your name a few times and went through to your website. You have no idea whether social media played a part or not. In this case, it's worth asking them if they follow you on social media. It will at least give you some indication as to whether your social media activity played a part in their decision. However, it could be that there are times when you just don't know.

It is much easier to track this if you sell online. Through setting up tracking links that you share via social media (you can do this via Google URL Builder to then see the clicks on your tracking link on Google Analytics), and with goals and conversions set up on your Google Analytics account (for example, if someone has gone to your 'thank you for your order' page then you know they have made a purchase), you should be able to see the customer journey of arriving at your site via social media and then making a purchase.

You can also track leads that come through social media. A lead might be someone who fills in your lead capture form on a squeeze page, a result of you sending them to that page via social media. Your Google Analytics will allow you to see how many people filled in that lead capture form via social media (again by looking at the number of people that ended up on your 'thank you for signing up' page). You then need to ensure you know your numbers. How many leads convert to customers on average and what is the typical lifetime value of a customer?

Measuring certainly isn't simple, but it IS worth doing, as once you know what is working and what isn't, you can start to see where to make changes or enhance the good bits, and begin to really smash your social media aims! So, set yourself up a spreadsheet, or whatever your preferred method is of logging the information, and make sure you measure your activity at the end of every month.

7.2. Social Media Return on Investment

Measuring the return on investment (ROI) of any marketing activity is rarely easy, but it's particularly difficult when it comes to social media.

To measure return on investment, there are two things you need to know:

1. How much money you spent
2. How much money you made

While social media may appear to be 'free', it certainly isn't! Here are a few costs that can be incurred from your social media activity.

- Your time – work out the hours you spend working on social media, and work out your hourly rate from your salary. Hourly rate x hours spent on social media = cost of time on social media. Make sure you track the time you spend on social media so that you can analyse this. Tracking time also ensures you don't end up procrastinating on social media, and seeing what celebrities and your friends are up to!
- Tools – many of the tools used for social media incur an element of cost. Have a look at the tools you use and whether you are paying for any, such as a monthly subscription to Buffer.
- Design – have you commissioned a designer to create imagery for you for social media? What was the cost?
- Photography – have you used a photographer to create images for social media use?
- Videography – have you used a videographer to create videos for social media use?
- Advertising – have you done any paid forms of advertising on social media?

- Competition prizes – have you invested in prizes to give away in social media competitions?
- Plus, any additional costs. Analyse all your activity and work out if there are other costs incurred within it.

Then there is the more fun and rewarding side – the return!! There are a few things you need to consider in terms of how much money you have made through social media.

- Sales – can you track the sales made directly through social media? It will be difficult to analyse ROI if you can't. Use tracking links and Google Analytics to help understand the online sales generated via social media. If you don't sell online, be sure to ask each customer how they heard of you. Or, give an offer code via social media only, so you know that they must have seen your update to know of the offer.
- Leads – if you are generating leads through social media, then you need to know your lead numbers. How many leads do you need to get one customer? For example, you might calculate that, on average, every 70 leads results in one customer.
- Lifetime value of a customer – of course, you would hope that once a customer has purchased from you the first time, they will buy from you again at some point in the future. You will need to work out the lifetime value of a customer to your business. This means calculating the average lifetime spend of a customer.

Once you have these figures in place, the next stage is to work out the ROI. The formula for calculating ROI percentage is:

ROI = (Income generated – costs incurred) / costs incurred x 100%

Let's work through an example. A sportswear company ran a campaign over a month on social media. At the end of the month they wanted to work out the return on investment of their campaigns.

COSTS INCURRED:

- Hours – they calculated that one employee spent 20 hours on the social media activity over that month. That employee's salary is £24,000. They work 5 days a week, for 8 hours a day. Their approximate hourly rate is £11.54. The total hourly labour cost was £230.80
- Tools – the company pays for Hootsuite each month at a cost of $9.99/month. Approximate conversion to GBP is £8.04
- Design – a designer was commissioned to create some graphics for the campaign at a total cost of £350
- Advertising – the company invested in Facebook Ads, at a total cost for the month of £1650

TOTAL COSTS INCURRED OVER THE MONTH: £2238.84

INCOME GENERATED:

- Sales – through selling online, the company could track that they generated £4375 in sales over the month
- Lifetime value of the customer – they know that, on average, the lifetime value of a customer is £249. They brought in 175 new customers via the campaign, who made their first purchase directly resulting from the campaign. If we take away the £25 purchase from their lifetime value, each customer will be worth on average an extra £224 to the company in the future. 175x224=£39,200

INCOME GENERATED: 4375+39200=£43,575

Now to calculate the return on investment.

ROI = (43575 - 2238.84) / 2238.84 x 100% = 1846%

That's a huge return on investment and a very successful campaign for the company. Of course, it does take on the lifetime value of the customer, which could be affected by future events, such as change in economies or the company being affected by bad PR. Or even the company ceasing to trade. However, it is important to consider the lifetime value, as this gives a true ROI for the campaign.

Even if we only worked out the ROI based on the sales directly made through it, the ROI is still 95%. A campaign that broke even, would generate a ROI of 0, and one that made a loss would lead to a negative result. So, 95% is still a good result!

I know I've gone in to this in detail, but it is important to understand and to start calculating ROI. Without it, you could be losing money through social media or, even better, you might not realise just what amazing results you are having!

7.3. Social Media Insights and Analytics

Each of the social media platforms offer some form of analytics to help you understand your activity on that platform. At a simple level, they will give you details of how many followers you have on that platform and the percentage growth in this. They will also show you the performance of each of your posts, showing you the reach and how many people engaged with that post. This is very important for seeing what posts are working well for your audience, and the posts that did not interest them. Use this information to guide your future posts.

You can analyse growth in engagement, comments, likes, shares/retweets, and other analytics that you wish to measure. You can also look at who your audience is, such as age, gender and location, and on LinkedIn company pages aspects such as seniority, industry and function. Explore each platforms analytics and work out the measures that you want to log each month.

Unfortunately, there are no analytics for your LinkedIn personal profile, other than analysing the people who are looking at your profile. If you wish to measure engagement on your personal LinkedIn status updates, and track increase in connections, you will need to measure these yourself.

7.4. Google Analytics

Tracking visits to your website from social media is a good measure of how well your social media is working. The assumption can be made that if your website visits from social media are increasing, you're doing something right! Though of course, you will need to track conversions from their visit (e.g. did they complete your contact form, fill in a lead capture, or buy from you?) to ensure that you are truly seeing success from those website visits.

Google Analytics is a great free tool for analysing website visits. If you are not already using Google Analytics, you will need to sign up and add some code to your website, to be able to track activity. There is a social tab on Google Analytics, which will show you your activity that has originated from a social media platform. It will breakdown the platforms and how many visitors you have had from that platform, within the period being analysed.

You can also delve deeper into aspects such as which pages are visited most from that platform, the visitor behaviour and numbers of new versus unique visitors. This is something you should be reviewing on a month by month basis, at the very least, and should form part of your monthly social media activity log.

7.5. Social Media Measurement Tools

There are lots of tools available to help you measure your social media activity. These range greatly in price. Most ask you to pay a monthly subscription fee to use the software, while others will create software based specifically around your business for an annual fee. The more you pay, it is likely the more the software will tell you. This can range from the simple analytics that are available to you for free via each platform, such as increase in followers, mentions, shares, etc. While others will go in to greater detail, including aspects such as sentiment and brand mentions.

Both Hootsuite and Buffer, that have been mentioned previously with regards to scheduling your content, allow you to analyse link clicks as well as engagement with your updates. Sprout Social is often recommended as a good social media analysis tool, giving you analytics on Facebook, Twitter and Instagram. This will give you the main analytics that you have access to via the platforms, as well as hashtag analysis, social listening and trends, depending on the package you opt for. Sprout Social also allows you to manage your social media, scheduling updates and responding to engagement. Sprout Social packages start at $99/month.

Other tools that you may wish to look in to with regards measurement include:

- Keyhole – measure a brand or trend's impact on Twitter, Facebook and Instagram
- Agorapulse – measure engagement analytics
- Brandwatch – position within market on social media and reputation
- BuzzSumo – search for keywords and content, and who's talking about them
- CrowdWatch – engagement data

- Edgar – tracks engagement
- Klout – understand your social media influence
- Quintly – measure against competitors
- Simply Measured – use of your website from social media visitors and social media analytics
- Socialbakers – extensive social media analytics
- Social Mention – keyword search

There are many, many, more tools available to help you measure your social media activity, with new ones being created all the time. Be sure to subscribe to some of the top social media blogs (such as Social Media Examiner) to be kept aware of new tools.

7.6. CASE STUDY – POLYMER SOLUTIONS

Polymer Solutions are a business-to-business focused US-based independent testing company, testing a range of materials for chemical composition, durability and safety. Hootsuite have highlighted how Polymer Solutions have used Hootsuite to measure and improve their social media activity (you can see the full case study at https://hootsuite.com/resources/polymer-solutions-social-media-case-study).

Polymer Solutions use Hootsuite's analytical tools to track follower increases, as well as click rates to help understand what is most relevant to their audience. They measured a 375% increase in follower growth with the help of Hootsuite's analytics. They've also tracked that their reach has expanded from local to global. With regular measurement, Polymer Solutions have been able to adapt the messages they share on social media to make them as relevant to their audience as possible, and have the data to prove that this is working.

Tools are really useful in helping to measure your social media activity. Identifying the right one for your business starts with understanding what you want to measure, as well as the budget you have in place for that measurement. Of course, measurement is irrelevant without improvement. So, use the data effectively to understand where you could be making improvements with your social media activity. Measurement is an ongoing process. Once improvements have been made, highlight their success and where there is room for further improvement.

7.7. SUMMARY

- Measurement is important to know what is working and what isn't, and if you are achieving your objectives and hitting your key performance indicators
- Social media return on investment (ROI) can be difficult to calculate. Where you can quantify costs and income from social media, you should then calculate your ROI
- Each platform has analytics that will show you your main social media analytics, such as follower numbers and reach
- You can use Google Analytics to analyse your website traffic from social media
- Other tools are available, such as Sprout Social, which will give you indepth analytics

WANT MORE?

You can download a social media measurement spreadsheet template at www.samflynn.co.uk/bookresources.

CHAPTER 8

SOCIAL MEDIA ADVERTISING

8.1. Social Media Advertising

Most social media platforms now offer businesses some way in which they can pay to advertise on that platform. Advertising on social media is a whole book itself! So, I won't be going in to every detail within this book, but I will give you some guidance as to what works well when it comes to advertising on social media.

The first step you must consider is which platform to advertise on. It goes without saying that this will be dependent on who you are trying to target with the advert. You should also consider how likely they are to be receptive to your advert on that platform. For example, you can target HR Managers on Facebook. But will HR Managers be receptive to an advert for a new people management system on Facebook? Or, are they more likely to respond positively to that advert on LinkedIn?

You also need to consider how likely someone is to take the action you require them to on a mobile device. The predominant use of social media is on mobile rather than desktop. If you require them to take many steps once they have clicked on your ad, you may be better sharing your ad to desktop only.

Return on investment (ROI) is very important when it comes to advertising. You will need a means by which to track the activity from your advert to your site. You may want to analyse actual spend or leads generated. If your ad is focused on increasing leads, you will need to know your numbers to understand the ROI of your ad. How many leads do you need to be able to generate one customer? What is the average lifetime value of a customer?

Ads can quickly become a big drain of money if you do not keep track of their activity. You may find you are getting a high volume of clicks but no sign ups or sales. By monitoring your adverts regularly, you can decide whether the advert needs editing, removing altogether, or whether to increase spend on those adverts that are performing well.

8.2. Promoted Posts

The simplest way to advertise your business on Facebook is via the boosted post option. Boosting a post is paying to display that post to a larger audience. With high-reach often being difficult to achieve, as discussed earlier, this can be an ideal way of getting your update on more timelines. The boost option sits underneath the post once it has been published to your page.

You are given the following audience targeting options when boosting your post:

1. Showing the post to those who like your page
This is great for getting back in the visibility of those who no longer engage with your content.

2. Showing the post to people who like your page and their friends
This allows you to get back in the visibility of your audience, while opening yourself up to new audience members, who may share similar qualities to your current audience.

3. Showing the post to people you choose through targeting
This allows you to target your post to those who fit the demographic targeting you have outlined. You can create your audience from demographics including location, age, gender and interests.

4. Showing the post to people who have visited your website
If you have the Facebook website pixel installed on your site, you can target your post to people who have visited your website.

You can choose to run your promotion on Instagram as well (as Facebook owns Instagram).

You will then make the decision of how much you want to pay to boost your post. The more you pay, the more people Facebook will show that post to. As you adjust your budget, Facebook will give you an idea of the estimated reach of that post based on that budget. You can choose how long you want your post to be boosted for, and Facebook will spread your budget over this timeframe. You must pay at least £1 per day for each boosted post. You are paying for impressions of your boosted post rather than clicks. So, the total amount you spend will not be affected by people clicking on your boosted post.

Once you have inputted your payment details, you will then submit your post to be boosted. This will go through Facebook's approval process. Be sure to read Facebook's advertising guidelines to understand more about what may or may not be approved.

Boosted posts work well for:

- Competitions
- Lead captures
- Offers and promotions
- And anything you want to be read/seen by a bigger audience, such as a blog post you have written

You can similarly decide to promote a post on Instagram, if you have a business Instagram profile and it is linked to a Facebook page. On LinkedIn, you can sponsor content from your company page to appear on the LinkedIn timelines of more users. On Twitter, you can also choose to promote a tweet you have posted when designing your advert.

8.3. Running Adverts

Adverts are slightly different to boosted posts. These cannot be quickly created from the business page, and you will need to go in to the ads manager for that platform to create the ad. A typical ad on all platforms includes at least one image (on some platforms you can add multiple images) or a video, a headline and some body text, and a call to action. In many cases, clicking on the ad will take the user through to a webpage.

On creating your ad, most platforms will ask you what your objective is and this will form the basis of your ad. Objectives include increasing followers, targeting local people, converting people from a webpage, and many others. Explore the options and determine the most appropriate objective for your advert.

When advertising, remember that you are still 'invading' their social media space. You may now also be targeting people who have never heard of your business before, and have not chosen to hear about it. Keep this in mind when forming your advert. Avoid being to sales-focused and instead try to pique their interest by being as relevant to them as possible. The more relevant an advert is to a user, the more likely they are to click on it and take the action required.

At all times have your target audience in mind. If your target audience is very broad, you may wish to break it down in to groups and deliver different adverts to different groups within your target audience.

Each platform has numerous options in terms of where your ad is displayed. For example, you could choose to only show you ad on mobile, or only on desktop. You could decide that you want it to appear within the home feed, or that you would prefer it to appear in a side column.
Work through the options slowly, ensuring you have picked the best possible solution for your objective.

8.4. Choosing Your Campaign Audience

Social media advertising can become very costly if you do not have your targeting right. Without the correct targeting, your ad will be showing to people who are less likely to become customers. They may click out of interest, costing you money with no return. This is where knowing your target audience inside and out is a real advantage.

Firstly, you will need to consider the simple demographics, such as age, gender and location. Then you will need to delve deeper in to the individual. What are their interests? What are their online behaviours? The more you can understand your target audience, the more refined you will be able to make your targeting.

Facebook will use more than just an individual's profile information to allow you to target them. Facebook gathers information on users via both mobile and desktop. When a user is logged in to Facebook, Facebook can monitor their activity on the web. It gives them a greater insight in to the individual, what interests them, and their behaviours. The information will also be based on their Facebook activity, such as the pages they like and engage with.

You can go into detail with Facebook targeting that is not as detailed on other platforms. For example, you could market to parents of children of certain ages, or to people who have a birthday or anniversary coming up, or those who are more likely to buy online.

You can also advertise to people who have visited your website, by including the Facebook advertising tracking pixel on the back end of your website. You can upload a list of customers' emails, and Facebook will advertise to those who have the same email address as their Facebook login. You can create a lookalike audience from this list too, of people with similar demographics and qualities as your customer list. You can also target people who have viewed your videos on Facebook.

Some of the same opportunities for targeting are present on Twitter, such as list upload and targeting website visitors, but the interest and behaviours are not quite as in-depth as those on Facebook. In addition, on Twitter, you can target a user based on who they follow, or keywords they have mentioned within tweets.

It's also important to remember to exclude those you don't want your advert being displayed to. With each additional interest or behaviour you add, you are expanding rather than limiting your audience. Think of interests and behaviours you wish to exclude. For example, you may not want your advert to be visible to people with a lower income level.

There are so many opportunities to get your audience right when it comes to advertising. Which makes it even more important to understand exactly who your audience is.

8.5. Bidding on Social Media Adverts

Most platforms will require you to bid for your advert to be seen. Let's take the most popular social media advertising platform, Facebook, as an example. You've decided to create an advert targeting women in the UK, aged under 35, who are engaged to be married. Firstly, there will be businesses who have set up adverts with the same targeting demographics. Then there will be businesses who want to advertise to any gender in the UK under 35, there will be those who want to target women in the UK of any age, there will be those who are targeting women interested in interiors (and some engaged women under 35 maybe!), and so on.

Essentially, one person is likely to be targeted by adverts from lots of different businesses for varying reasons. Facebook can't show all the adverts to everyone in that target audience, or there will be nothing but ads on Facebook, and we'd all leave! As such, you will need to bid against these other businesses for your advert to be seen.

Bidding means you outline how much you are prepared to pay either per click on your advert (CPC) or how much you are prepared to pay for every 1000 impressions of your advert (CPM). Choosing to bid on clicks is often the best approach when you first create your advert. That way, you are only paying if someone is interested enough to actually click on your advert, rather than paying for someone to see your ad. If you are experiencing high volumes of clicks on your ad, you may then want to switch to CPM to reduce the amount you pay (this is why you need to monitor your adverts!).

Each platform will give you a suggested bid range. Or you can choose for that platform to choose your bid. While letting the platform choose your bid may result in your ad being more visible, it could cost you considerably more than keeping control of it yourself. Always better to be in control, I think! When controlling the bidding yourself, start at the upper range of the suggested bid, and consider going above it. This will ensure deliverability of your ad, giving you data straight away as to how your ad is performing and whether you could improve it. You can then reduce your bid once you have this information.

Let's run an example. Facebook has given you a suggested bid range of £2.05 - £2.85 per click based on the audience you wish to target. You might then consider bidding £3.00 per click for the first few hours of your ad being live, for it to be as visible as possible and give you information on its success. You could then gradually reduce the bid, taking it down to the top end of the range initially, and then step-by-step reducing it until you see a drop-off in deliverability. You will not necessarily have to pay the top end of your bid amount. Facebook will charge you dependent on the other bids made for that target audience, but will not go over your bid amount.

There are agencies that can manage your social media advertising campaigns, and it is clear to see why! The more time and monitoring you give your adverts, with changes made where needed, the more successful (with a greater ROI) they will be.

8.6. Your Advert Visuals

How your advert look can have a big impact on the success of your advert. The image is likely to be the most important aspect of your ad. Without an image that draws attention to your ad, the ad is unlikely to perform well. Black and white options often perform well, as they stand out from the colourful feed. And pictures of people often work better than graphics. They fit better within social media feeds. Don't include too much text within your image. Facebook will not allow images with greater than 20% of the image being text.

You can also use video within your advert. Make sure you include subtitles, as many people will view your ad without audio. As videos will autoplay, this instantly draws a user's eye to the advert. You can gather a large number of video views for a relatively low cost.

Be sure to think about the other aspects of the ad too. The headline should be as relevant as possible to the person you are hoping to see the ad. Include relevant information in the headline such as location or interest. This will draw the subconscious attention of the user, as it includes something that is relevant to them.

You can create a display link that is different to the link you are sending clicks to. For example, I may have the following link to send people to when promoting my workshops: www.samflynn.co.uk/upcomingworkshops. But to look more appealing and simple, I use samflynn.co.uk as the display link.

The text should be to the point and only include information that is relevant or likely to encourage a user to click on the ad. You may also include something here that discourages users from clicking on an ad. For example, adding a date to an event advert may discourage those unable to make that date from clicking the ad and costing you more money.

And finally, the call to action should be relevant to the action you wish the user to take. Make it as simple as possible for them. If you want them to buy, the call to action should be 'buy now'. If you are sending them to something giving them more information, it should be 'learn more'.

8.7. Trialling Different Adverts

A big mistake to make when advertising on social media is to produce just one advert. You can create many adverts under the same campaign, that the platform will then rotate delivery of for you. The adverts will fall under the same budget, so creating several adverts will not cost you more money.

The reason behind creating several adverts is to test what works best for your audience. By creating only one advert, we have nothing to compare it against. It may perform poorly when compared to an alternative advert.

When split-testing different adverts, you are working towards creating a 'super advert'. One that works best for your audience. You will be able to highlight the elements that work best within each advert. As such, you should only change one element within each advert.

Start by creating your first advert. Then, with your second, change just one element, such as the image. You could even create several more adverts that are all identical except for the image used. You will then be able to see which image performed best. You can do the same for the headline and the body text, and any other elements that are present within your ad. You could test these different adverts for 3-5 days, then use the information to create a 'super advert' that has all the elements that performed best, and run this advert for a longer period.

When testing your advert, you are looking for that which delivers the best outcome. For example, generates the most sales or leads. You are not looking for the advert that is clicked on the most. Clicks are a good indicator of whether the advert has piqued interest, but if the sales or leads aren't coming through, it's not meeting its objective. It could be that the ad is misleading, and they don't want to make the purchase after clicking the ad, for example. Make sure you have conversion tracking in place to allow you to analyse the advert that has worked best.

Trialling different ads in this way will ensure you get the best outcome from your adverts, and you'll know what's working to help you create even better adverts in the future.

8.8. Measuring Advert Success

You should never run an advert 'for the sake of it'! There always needs to be a clear objective for why you are running your advert. This should then translate in to how you are measuring the success of that advert. The ROI of your ad campaign could be as simple as the income generated compared to the cost of the campaign. However, it's also worth taking in to account additional costs, such as cost of imagery, time to create and manage the ad campaign and any other costs that can be directly attributed to that campaign. You also need to consider that income may go beyond that directly generated from the campaign. For example, what is the lifetime value of a customer? They may have spent £10 directly, as a result of your campaign, but you may know that the average lifetime value of a customer is actually £250, which can have a big impact on ROI.

Each platform has an advert management area, which will highlight key data for your adverts, such as number of clicks and engagement rates. Make sure you are tracking as much as you possibly can from your ad campaign. Add the tracking pixels available on many of the social media platforms, as these will track not just spend from directly clicking on the ad, but also any additional spend within a set timeframe after clicking on the ad. If you cannot directly track income from your campaign, consider tracking leads generated, or another measure that will give you an indication of how many customers you are likely to generate from your campaign.

Success in advertising comes down to constant monitoring and improvement. Don't just discount ever using an advert that delivered a poor or negative ROI for your business. Instead, consider why this might have been the case and how you can avoid it in the future. Analyse the factors behind the success of those that deliver a great ROI, so that you can repeat this going forward. Advertising on social media can lead to great success for businesses when they get it right.

But it can also be very costly. Be sure to measure your success to ensure you're making, rather than wasting, money.

8.9. CASE STUDY – NORTHUMBRIA UNIVERSITY

Twitter have shared the success that Northumbria University have achieved in running Twitter advertising campaigns. Their main goal was to increase course applications. To do this with Twitter adverts, they focused on a website clicks campaign to drive traffic through to their application process.

Northumbria University tried several variations of their messaging to see what worked best within their adverts, then updated campaigns as they went along to make them as successful as possible. They made changes to both images and copy to highlight what would create the most successful advert.

They found the targeting that was most successful for them was using a Tailored Audience, loading their existing prospect list, and then marketing to this list via Twitter adverts. They also remarketed to people who had visited their website. They used images of students wearing the Northumbria hoodie in their adverts, to allow the audience to relate to becoming a student there.

The result was that they were 50% below their target for cost-per-engagement, allowing them to take more applications at a lower cost.

How could you emulate Northumbria University's advertising success? Do you have a large prospect email list that you could market to via social media? Or, could you target those who have visited your website? There are opportunities for every business when it comes to social media advertising, so consider the best approach for yours and give it a go!

8.10. SUMMARY

- Social media advertising is a great way to get your message in front of a larger, highly targeted audience
- Promoted posts allow you to pay to get your content seen by more people. You can opt for this to be seen by your current audience, or to target a new audience
- Social media adverts typically include one image (or multiple on some platforms), a headline, body text, a call to action and a link
- You will need to choose your audience. Think about the exact audience your advert is aimed at, and who are most likely to respond positively to it
- You will bid the amount you are willing to pay per click or per 1000 impressions of your ad. You are bidding against other advertisers
- Think about the advert visuals that will appeal most to your target audience
- Trial different adverts to determine the features that are most successful
- Measure the success of your adverts to determine campaign success and return on investment, and whether something needs adapting in future to increase success

WANT MORE?

You can download a '10 Things To Promote In Social Media Adverts' ideas list over at www.samflynn.co.uk/bookresources.

CHAPTER 9

YOUR SOCIAL MEDIA ACTIONS

9.1. YOUR SOCIAL MEDIA ACTIONS

Of course, reading a book on a subject doesn't magically lead you to have greater success in that area. The success comes from taking action and implementing what you have learned. This book is either just the start of, or part of, your journey towards social media success. I hope you've made lots of notes throughout the book and highlighted actions you need to take.

It's time to put your action plan in place. Start with a list of ten actions you wish to make to help you on your way to social media success. Then prioritise them. Finally, give them deadlines to action them. Start with the highest priority and work your way down to the lowest. Trying to do everything at once can often lead to doing it all poorly. Focusing on one aspect at a time, then moving to the next when that is completed, will lead to more success.

Your social media learning shouldn't end here. Social media is constantly changing and there are new ways of doing things, and some of the old ways are sometimes removed (worst nightmare if you've just written a book about them!!). So, keep up to date by subscribing to social media blogs, and the blogs of the platforms themselves. This should keep you in the loop about new things you can do on the platforms.

Most of all, social media is SOCIAL, and socialising should always be fun. So, go have some fun. And, of course, lots of success too!

9.2. SUMMARY

- You will only achieve social media super success when you take the relevant actions needed
- Create an action list
- Prioritise your actions and set deadlines
- Keep up to date by subscribing to social media blogs
- Have fun and lots of success
- Good luck!!

WANT MORE?

There is an action plan template to download at www.samflynn.co.uk/bookresources. No excuses, go fill it in now!!

FOLLOW SAM

If you've any questions about the book or social media, or anything else I can help you out with, social media is probably the place to do it!

Come follow me and say hi!

Facebook:	www.facebook.com/samflynnsocialmedia
Twitter:	www.twitter.com/_samflynn
Instagram:	www.instagram.com/samflynnsm
LinkedIn:	www.linkedin.com/in/samflynn
YouTube:	www.youtube.com/samflynnsocialmedia

23698996R00103

Printed in Poland
by Amazon Fulfillment
Poland Sp. z o.o., Wrocław